Black Flag

A Coding Club Mission

By Matt Langley

In collaboration with Chris Roffey

CAMBRIDGE
UNIVERSITY PRESS

University Printing House, Cambridge CB2 8BS, United Kingdom

Cambridge University Press is part of the University of Cambridge.

It furthers the University's mission by disseminating knowledge in the pursuit of education, learning and research at the highest international levels of excellence.

www.cambridge.org
Information on this title: www.cambridge.org/9781107671409

© Matt Langley 2014

First published 2014

Printed in Poland by Opolgraf

A catalogue record for this publication is available from the British Library

ISBN 978-1-107-67140-9 Paperback

Additional resources for this publication at www.cambridge.org/codingclub-blackflag

Cover image: ©Tihomir Tikulin, Beehive Illustration Ltd

Acknowledgements

Nothing can survive in a vacuum, never mind flourish. I am indebted to a lot of very good people who make me look much better than I am, to Stephanie, Kate, Heather, Jennie, Jilly, Jo, Tico, Berenice and my partner in crime, Chris, I couldn't imagine a better bunch of anarchists to have fight the system at my side!

Introduction

This is not a traditional novel. Matt Langley's *Black Flag: A Coding Club Mission* enables you to take your reading experience a step further by allowing you to interact with the story via the free companion website www.cambridge.org/codingclub-blackflag.

Computer programmers come in many forms: male or female, young or old, good or evil. When they get started in front of a keyboard their skills can easily look like magic to the untrained eye. However, unlike magic, the knowledge and skills of programming are not cloaked in secrecy, the opposite in fact, they are well within your grasp.

Join the characters in *Black Flag* as they journey through the world that has been forced upon them. The characters have to solve problems, break codes and decipher hidden messages, often under extreme pressure, but they do so with skill, skills that you too can learn and master.

As you read through this novel look out for the prompts for the accompanying website.

 Whenever you see this symbol you can join Danni, one of the characters, online to solve coding challenges and take the next step in completing your mission.

Enjoy the puzzles but don't get disheartened if you find them difficult; our characters are not facing easy challenges and neither are you. There will be hints provided to help you along the way. If you get really stuck all of the passwords can be found at the back of the book, but be warned, all of the passwords are supplied in code: we don't want them falling into the wrong hands. The website FAQ section provides details on how to decode them. Remember, there is never just one correct way of solving these puzzles. In these desperate situations, more often than not, finding a solution, any solution, is all that matters.

Right now though, there is a lot to do and the citizens of New Edgehill are in need of your help. Before we go any further Danni has a message for you and has your first puzzle! Solve the puzzle and obtain your username and password to access the website.

Hidden Login
Difficulty: ✳

*I must keep this short, you can trust us! We know what is going on. To get involved with the movement yourself, you will need to **open your eyes**. Go to the website, you'll find the URL at the front of the book, keep it safe. This is an initiation. I can't take the risk of writing the password down. You have to find it yourself, so think like a true hacker: ignore the visuals and dig into the code.*

Once you are in, fill in the form; it will allow us to keep track of your progress and provide you with many of the resources and tools that we use to fight against this oppression.

Keep safe and good luck!
Danni

Chapter 1

It was a black and white world. It didn't matter how many
shades of the spectrum coloured it; it would always be black
and white. Black and white. Nothing in between. Especially
when it came to something like war.

The screen flashed from one conflict zone to another. Cal
Jones couldn't tear his eyes away. He wasn't an idiot, but even
he couldn't tell them apart. The banner text beneath the pictures

proclaimed exotic locations like New Rio, New Delhi, New York. All places that were bright, shiny and, as their names promised, new. He had heard of them, of course. Who hadn't? But he knew he'd never get to visit them, any more than he'd get to visit places with real history, like Old Lichfield or Old Amsterdam or Old Venice. They were just names to him.

12:59.

In less than a minute the entire city would stop as the clock struck thirteen and the CyberCore International news stream would start, bringing everyone up to date with the latest efforts of the security forces as they moved to protect the borders.

This was Cal's route home. Every day at the same time he stood in the square watching the news stream.

Words scrolled across his brain: *fear, terror, threat, the enemy, out there, always, circling, watching, waiting, trust no one, be vigilant, be a good Citizen.* It was on a permanent loop now. *Fear, terror . . . be vigilant.* Cal had lived with that message all his life. They all had. It was as if the images carried subliminal messages that pumped right into his brain. Around him people began to slow down, taking up positions at the street corner and along the pavement to get a better view of the infoscreens that dominated the huge plaza. Cal gripped the shoulder strap of his rucksack, doing his best to prevent the contents from being squashed in the crush as people jostled for position. No one wanted to miss a thing.

The infoscreen filled with a clock face, its red second hand sweeping round to join the hour and the clock struck thirteen. The street around Cal fell utterly silent; every single car idled as every traffic light turned red for the broadcast. It was as though the entire world held its breath.

'Greetings, Citizens of New Edgehill.' The image of the clock morphed flawlessly into the craggy face of Marshall Trent. He stared down on every centimetre of the city like a god. Cal thought he looked a little older today, a few more lines round his eyes maybe, a few more creases on his forehead, but he knew that they should all be grateful he was looking after them. The world needed men like Marshall Trent.

'Today I bring grave news,' Marshall Trent said, his voice filling their ears thanks to their implants. They were all connected via their Neurochips. A constant ebb and flow of data that transformed humanity into one great hive mind. 'There has been an attack on our Exploratory Outpost in Bright Town. The extent of the casualties is not known at this time, but an official list will be accessible within the hour. This is the third such cowardly attack in the last month and our heart goes out to those who have lost loved ones in these trying times. But I have a message for these fearmongers, a promise: we will find you and you will be brought to justice. We shall not rest until every last one of you is in custody. We shall not sleep until peace is restored. You have our word. Your days are numbered.'

There was silence as Trent's promise filtered through the crowd. Cal saw the adoration in his fellow pedestrians' faces as they gazed up at the screens all around them. Marshall Trent was watching over them. Marshall Trent would keep them safe.

'War continues to rage in many Communities of the world,' Trent continued, 'and while our troops stand by in readiness I will not needlessly put the lives of our brave young men and women in danger. We will not intervene unless given no choice. Sadly, I fear that our enemies intend to force our hand. I want each and every one of you to know that when the time comes we *will* fight. But more than that, we will win.'

Around his face, the earlier images of conflict were repeated, but instead of New Rio, New Delhi and New York, this time they were places Cal recognised, battle-scarred but unmistakable. 'These are landmarks we love and cherish,' said Trent. 'These are the places we will defend. Be vigilant.

You never know where the threat lies. It could be someone you know. It could be someone you love. It could be someone standing beside you. I want you to look at the person standing next to you right now, I want you to look at the person sitting in the cubicle alongside you, at the cash register in front of you. I want you to look to your neighbour. I want you to remember that where we feel safe, where we think we are surrounded by friends and loved ones, is where we are most vulnerable. We let our guard down. We give our enemies a place to hide close to our hearts. That is the ugly truth. Trust no one.'

Cal was all too aware of people turning their heads, looking suspiciously at each other. More than a few eyes stared at him. He felt his heart rate quicken. His eyes darted over the crowd. Surely it wasn't just because he was the youngest? Or maybe it was. He had done nothing wrong. But even so he held his bag tight, certain that someone was going to try to take it from him, demanding to know what was inside. He licked his lips. He could feel a bead of sweat trickle down the back of his neck.

'We have images of this morning's attack on the outpost –' And before anyone could look away the screen shifted to show a smoking building. It was impossible to tell what the damage was, or what had caused it. Cal stared at the ruin, shaking his head. How was he supposed to work out anything about the building from the picture? How were any of them meant to know where it was or what went on within its four walls? They only had Marshall Trent's word that this was the Exploratory Outpost in Bright Town. But that was enough. Trent would never lie to them.

'This was not the work of foreign agents. A group who call themselves the New Luddites were responsible for this cowardly attack. They want to destroy everything we have worked so hard to recreate after the Last Great Civil War. This is why I urge you to look closely at your friends and neighbours. This is why I urge you to look for any change in their behaviour, anything that might be deemed suspicious or out of character. Any clues to what they are thinking or planning. You might be the difference, my friends. Do not let these Anarchists destroy everything we have built.'

There was a collective gasp from the crowd as the picture changed to show a teenage boy lying on the ground.

The shaky camera moved closer.

A hand entered the shot, turning the boy's head to one side to reveal the extent of his wounds.

Cal did not know what shocked him more: that this boy might be dead or that someone had tampered with his Neurochip.

He touched his own ear. All around him others were doing the same. Of all the rules, of all the laws they lived their lives by, all the regulations that helped to keep their lives in order and kept them safe, one was sacrosanct: no one tampered with their Neurochip.

'These people flout the law,' Trent said, the anger in his voice barely disguised. 'I am urging you, my people, my *friends*, be vigilant. Watch for aberrant behaviour. Watch for people acting out of character. Watch for stray words that may give them away. Different is wrong. Remember that. We are a society. That means we are together. We are the same. Always. Alone we are weak. Together we are strong. Together we are *safe*.'

The screen showed another building, which could have been any building in any new town, though this time angry flames licked through its broken windows and black smoke poured out. The image flashed again, bringing up the image of the wound on the boy's neck. The message was clear. These people were capable of the unthinkable. They must be stopped.

The silence that had accompanied the news stream was quickly replaced by the hum of chatter as people realised that it was over.

In his head the war had always been happening somewhere else; the devastation was always an image on the big screens of some distant place, but it was obvious the threat was ever-present and closer than any of them wanted to admit. It could come to New Edgehill at any time. He'd grown up being told it was possible to be standing next to the enemy and not know it. That was how the Net Law worked, it relied upon people like him turning on their friends and neighbours and giving them up to the Enforcers. Cal was seventeen years old. In that time he'd come into contact with a lot of people. He had no way of knowing how many, but surely he must have encountered Anarchists hell-bent on bringing down Marshall Trent and ending his peace? That was Trent's message, wasn't it? They had all met Anarchists even if they didn't recognise them.

Cal turned away from the infoscreen and began to push his way through the dispersing crowd. Many of them wore the same stunned expression and seemed unable to move until the growing growl of the traffic meant that life was reasserting itself and they had no choice in the matter. Cal gripped the shoulder strap of his backpack and squirmed and wriggled and ducked between people, head down, until a huge roar of sound stopped everyone dead in their tracks again.

There was a moment of silence in the wake of the explosion where nothing existed, no sound, no air, nothing, and then the screams came.

Cal felt a rush of heat across his face as he looked up.

All around him people were panicking, pushing to get out of the square, anywhere away from the source of the explosion. They didn't know what it was or where it had happened. It didn't matter. It was close. It was enough to have them pulling and clawing at each other to get through gaps that weren't there. Car horns blared. Engines roared. And more screams. Always more screams.

Cal's head was spinning. He struggled to locate the source of the panic, but was caught in a tide of bodies that dragged him further away. Instead of going with them, he stood his ground, twisting and turning to let people surge round him like a rock at the bottom of a rushing river. His bag was torn from his shoulder. He barely managed to snatch it back before it was carried away in the press of people. Cal clutched it to his chest.

'Stop her!' someone shouted.

Cal couldn't see who had called out, or who they wanted stopped. He wasn't a tall boy. Sometimes that was a good thing, it meant he could slip by unnoticed when he wanted to, but at times like this it was a distinct disadvantage.

Space opened up around him. He saw corn-yellow hair streaked with a blaze of purple: a girl running flat out, weaving through traffic to a chorus of horns and screeching brakes. Judging by the trail of anger and confusion trailing in her wake, the girl had come from the Watchhouse on the far side of the plaza. She jumped, barely hurdling the wing of an Enforcer before it ploughed into her, and she came down on the bonnet and rolled away, on her feet again and running before the car had stopped moving.

Then Cal saw the Enforcer on her tail, its stun baton ready to strike her down. Cal could feel the sense of hunger from the crowd . . . they wanted this girl to pay for what she'd done – it didn't matter that they didn't know what she'd done, if anything. The Enforcer was chasing her. She was running. She must be one of the familiar enemies Marshall Trent had been talking about, the enemy within. Cal was frightened for her. There was no way this was going to end well.

She was no more than ten metres away from him when they made eye contact.

He realised two things. She was young, younger than him, probably a couple of years younger, though it was hard to tell through the blackened soot smears on her face. And she was scared.

As she bolted away from him the girl cast a frightened backwards glance at the Enforcer, and as she did her hair fell away from her neck and Cal saw an angry red smear of blood behind her ear where her Neurochip should have been. She was one of them.

The girl stumbled and for one sickening second Cal thought she was going to fall in front of the next car, but she sprang up, planting her hands on its bonnet and used it like a vault, her momentum carrying her up and over the front of the car.

The gymnastic manoeuvre left the Enforcer on the wrong side of the vehicle. It slammed into the side of the car, pushing it aside as though it wasn't there and went on relentlessly.

Cal had never seen an Enforcer in action, and given the way it had just brushed a ton of metal aside he hoped he'd never need to again. It closed the gap on the girl in the silence between two of Cal's heartbeats – it was that *fast*.

The Enforcer raised its baton and swung down hard. It was a stun baton, so it didn't need any power behind the swing, but the droid had chosen deadly force over simply stunning the girl. The impact would shatter her skull.

Without thinking Cal threw his backpack, its trajectory putting it between the girl's head and the Enforcer's lethal blow. The bag took the full impact of the droid's swing. He felt a sizzle of energy as a jolt of electricity ripped out of the baton and seared through the backpack, burning up his arm to his shoulder. The shock sent him spinning. By the time he'd caught his balance the girl had swept the legs out from under the Enforcer and scrambled back to her feet, leaving it flailing around on its back like an upended turtle.

Some of the Citizens had shaken themselves free of the shock and formed a vigilante wall.

Cal realised what he'd done. She was an Anarchist. He'd
saved an Anarchist's life. But as he looked at her, all he saw was
a girl. Marshall Trent's words about familiar enemies rang in
his ears as the crowd closed in on them, made brave by the fact
the Anarchist was only a girl. Even though they didn't know
what she'd done they weren't about to let her escape. Cal stood
between them. The way they looked at him was frightening.
There was so much hate in their eyes. Cal's mind was racing.
He'd risked his life to save her. She was an Anarchist. That
made him one too, didn't it? He'd broken the order of Marshall
Trent's peace. He'd prevented an Enforcer from bringing an
Anarchist to justice. That's why they looked like they wanted to
tear into him like rabid dogs.

'Run!' the girl screamed at Cal.

She didn't wait for him.

Chapter 2

Cal didn't need telling twice.

He ran as fast as his legs would carry him, head down and arms and legs pumping furiously, the backpack slapping against his legs until he hoicked it over his shoulder. He didn't dare slow down by even a single step. The temptation was to abandon it, but the contents were far too precious to throw away. Fresh fruit wasn't easy to lay your hands on. He'd been lucky today.

Not that being chased by an Enforcer because it thinks I'm an Anarchist is particularly lucky, he thought, panicking.

He could hear the mob behind them. All he wanted to do was get home, give the fruit to his father and make him smile. It wasn't a lot to ask, was it?

He followed the girl down a narrow alleyway that squirmed between two towering buildings. He kept casting frightened glances over his shoulder to see if the mob was gaining on them and every time he did she urged him to, *'Come on!'*

She ducked through an open doorway and pulled him in after her. Cal went sprawling across the ground.

She pushed the door closed, and stood with her back pressed against it, panting. In the darkness he could hear the drumming of his heart in his ears. It was *all* he could hear. He didn't move. He didn't dare make a sound.

The mob charged down the alleyway, cursing the Anarchists and swearing to tear them limb from limb if it laid hands on them, then surged past the closed door, taking its hatred with it.

Cal closed his eyes. He couldn't quite believe what had just happened.

'Thank you,' the girl said in between heavy gasps as she struggled to catch her breath.

He had no idea why he'd helped her, but he had, and now he was very much part of this. Whatever this was. Even if no one in the crowd had recognised him, the Enforcer would have his face stored, and it wouldn't take long to run facial recognition and pull his name and Personal Identifier, or PID, up from the Register, and then they'd know everything about him: where he lived, where he went to school, his grades, and from that they'd get to everything else – his browsing habits, the search strings he'd run when he'd been trying to find out more about the war, the banned books he'd got stored on his cloud drive. He'd have no secrets. And as long as he had the Neurochip in his head they'd be able to reprogram the curiosity out of him.

If he lived that long.

Now he was frightened.

'I should go home,' he said, 'Dad's alone . . .'

He pushed himself unsteadily to his feet, and slung the backpack back on to his shoulder. He couldn't see her in the darkness, but he knew from her silence she didn't think it was a good idea. He didn't know what else to do. 'You think I should wait a little longer? They might come back.'

'They *will* come back,' she said. 'And as long as you've got that thing in your head they'll always be able to find us wherever we hide. But we can't just sit here.'

She pushed something into his hands.

'It's a baseball cap,' she said, sensing his confusion. 'Put it on. It'll interfere with the signal from your chip.'

Cal did as he was told.

Something scraped against his skin. The inside of the cap wasn't fabric. It felt like lead foil. It dug into his neck uncomfortably. No doubt that was how it inhibited the signal.

She pushed it all the way down on to his head. 'Sorry. Can't take any chances.'

'What are you talking about?'

Marshall Trent was right, these people were dangerous. They all were, these Anarchists. Tin-foil hats? Every conspiracy theorist in New Edgehill would punch the air in victory. He shook his head.

'They know who you are already,' she said. 'You know that, don't you? The Enforcer scanned your chip the moment you broke the Net Law and helped me. Your details have been disseminated to every Enforcer in the city, every Drone in the sky. You're on the list. You're an Anarchist. You are an enemy of Marshall Trent. They're looking for you.'

'But I . . . I didn't do anything . . . I'll just explain . . .' Cal started to say, hearing how pathetic it sounded before he'd even finished saying it. No one would believe him.

'The baseball cap will block the signal for now, but we have to do something more permanent.'

'What do you mean "more permanent"?' But he knew. He'd seen the scar behind her ear. It was the scar that had marked the dead Anarchist on the news stream. That little red smear of blood behind their ears was suddenly the most important thing in the whole world.

'You can't go back. Your old life is over,' she said, and as much as he didn't want to, he believed her. 'It was the minute you saved me from the Enforcer's baton.' She shook her head. Cal looked at her properly for the first time. Yes she was young, yes she looked like the cute pixieish girl next door without the freckles, but there was something about her eyes. She seemed so much older than him when he looked into them. 'I thought you knew . . . I thought you were one of us . . . I thought that was why you did it.'

'I didn't know anything. I still don't.'

'I'm so sorry . . . If you go back, they'll make an example of you for helping me. They'll brand you a familiar enemy and your face will become the face of the Anarchists. It'll be worse for your father, too. They'll think he was complicit. This way he can deny knowing you are an Anarchist.'

'But I'm not,' Cal said stubbornly.

'Try telling the Enforcers that. See if they listen. This way your dad'll have a chance at a normal life. If you go back, then he's harbouring an Anarchist. You know what the punishment for that is, don't you?'

He did.

How could a single act of kindness utterly destroy his life? All he'd done was try to stop her from being badly hurt. Surely that shouldn't be a crime? But, and this was an important realisation, even if he'd known what would happen Cal Jones would have done the same thing. It had been instinct. He hadn't had to think about it; his father had raised him well, and he knew the difference between right and wrong. What the Enforcer had been about to do was definitely wrong.

'So what am I supposed to do? Come with you?' Cal asked.

'Not while you've still got that thing in your head you're not,' she replied. 'I'm Sasha, by the way, pleased to meet you, whoever you are.'

'Cal,' he said. 'Callaghan Jones. My friends call me Cal.'

'Then Callaghan it is,' Sasha said, leading him out into the light.

Chapter 3

They tried not to run. Running got you noticed. That was the last thing they wanted. They tried not to be noticed, even though everyone seemed to be watching everyone else. At first they moved with the crowds, but then Sasha took him down to the river and led him beneath one of the bridges. Decent people stayed away from the bridges. A cardboard city had sprung up along the river. Outsiders gathered around braziers for warmth. These people had made a choice. They had chosen not to be part of the new world. They had put themselves on the outside. They had turned their backs on Marshall Trent's offers of help, housing and food. They were the underbelly. Cal had always been brought up to believe that there was nothing down here that ordinary decent Citizens needed be concerned with, and yet here he was. There must have been a hundred or more of these outsiders living along the riverbank in their makeshift settlement. It stank.

'You should be safe here for a while,' she said.

He didn't believe her.

'You're going to leave me, aren't you?'

She smiled at him. 'I need to fetch someone to deal with your Neurochip.'

'Can't you just take me to them?'

She shook her head. 'Too risky for Danni. Right now you're a big red arrow walking through the city.' She pointed at his neck. 'Your chip's a tracking device. As long as we don't know if they're tracing your signal it's best we be careful. The last thing I want to do is to lead the Enforcers to one of our safe houses. Trust me, *Cal*,' she said. 'I won't abandon you. I don't do that to friends.'

Cal nodded, thinking. 'What will he do?'

What he really meant was will it hurt? He couldn't shake the image of the boy on the screen. Had he died when they'd tried to extract his Neurochip?

'Danni'll burn it out.'

'Burn it? While it's still under my skin?'

'It doesn't hurt,' Sasha said, but Cal could tell she was lying. She wasn't a very good liar. 'It takes too long to cut one out. The Enforcers have aerial Drones ready to take out anyone tampering with their chip.' She was right, he'd seen them up there, they looked like magpies, black and white bodies with thin wings, but they weren't. Massive android warriors on the ground, deadly robot birds in the sky? It was the stuff of nightmares. 'Marshall Trent's got eyes everywhere. Burning the chip kills the signal before the Drones can pinpoint your location.'

'How do you know all this stuff? How do I know that you're not just making it all up?'

Sasha tapped her own neck. 'You think I would have had gone through with it if I wasn't absolutely sure what was being done to me? Trust me, Cal. I've seen what they're like first-hand. I've been inside several Watchhouses. There's a reason they all look the same, with a huge gothic tower, like a witch's finger pointing up at the sky, with data panels and dishes to receive the data flow from the *Neuralnet* instead of fingernails. They don't have many windows, you've noticed that, right? They don't want you seeing inside them. And do you know why? Because of what they do in there.'

That explained the source of the explosion. She'd bombed a Watchhouse.

'Why hit a Watchhouse? Don't they monitor what's going on in the rest of the world?'

Sasha laughed. It wasn't a harsh or unpleasant sound, but it made him feel small and naive. She was younger than him, but she acted as if she was so much more worldly wise. 'They're not interested in what's going on *outside* the Isles, Cal. They couldn't care less if the Chinese or the Indians or the South Americans are tearing each other apart. They don't care about the North Koreans, the South or the Americas. They're watching us! The Watchhouses are intel hordes. That's where they keep every single piece of data they've collected on us. Everything you do, everything you say or think ends up in one of those vast stores, processed by the machine. You haven't got any secrets, Cal. That's life in the Reunited Kingdom. That's our reality.'

The sound of a siren close by made Cal's mouth go dry. For a moment he thought that his heart was going to burst out of his chest, it was beating that fast, that hard. He pulled the brim of the baseball cap down a little further, making sure that the lead-foil lining covered the patch of skin behind his ear where the Neurochip was embedded. What Sasha was saying didn't make any sense. Why would Marshall Trent spy on his own people when there was so much happening out in the world that threatened to destabilise his hard won peace? Surely that was where his attention was focussed? Cal saw it on the news streams every day, the constant ebb and flow of battle reports streamed back from the frontlines while the Isles considered the cost of intervention. Marshall Trent valued his people. He didn't want to throw away their lives by getting involved in some bloody war he couldn't hope to win . . . Cal didn't have time to think about it, not now.

'Stay here,' she said. 'I'll be back.'

'How long will you be?' he asked, doing his best to hide the panic in his voice. It wasn't easy.

'Half an hour. Maybe a little more. You'll be safe here as long as you stay put. I promise.'

There was a change in her expression as if she had suddenly remembered something and didn't like what she'd remembered. 'Have you got a rig?'

'Of course.' It was a stupid question. Everyone had a rig. It was the easiest way of keeping in touch with people.

'Show me.' She held out her hand to take the handheld device from him. He did as he was told. She visibly relaxed as she looked at it. 'Has it always been switched off?'

'It's low on charge,' he said. 'There's enough juice to run some emergency protocols, but that's it.'

'Good. They could have tracked you through it. I can't believe I was so sloppy. We just got very lucky, Cal. Anything that broadcasts a signal can be traced.'

He didn't feel very lucky. He was hiding under a bridge waiting for someone to come and burn his Neurochip out. There was no going back from this. No explaining it as an innocent mistake. He'd be branding himself an enemy of the state. She might like living this way, she must have made the choice after all, but the only thing he'd decided to do was to stop her getting her head caved in by an Enforcer's baton and suddenly his life was being turned upside-down. He wanted to go home. Home was the one safe place everyone was supposed to have, wasn't it?

He didn't say anything as she slipped the rig into her pocket.

'I'll get rid of it,' Sasha said. 'I think I can buy us a little extra time and keep your father safe.' She got to her feet and scrambled up the embankment without so much as a backwards glance, and for the first time in his life Cal felt alone. Really alone. It didn't matter that there were a hundred other outsiders down here with him. Not one of them looked his way.

Chapter 4

She was gone far longer than Cal had expected. Time passed slowly. He'd done his best to make himself comfortable, climbing the bank of paving stones that rose five metres from the path and the cardboard city below, to where the bridge's first arch began above him, and wedging his back up against the concrete wall. The bridge was covered with an inventive spray of graffiti. He couldn't take his eyes off the cardboard boxes down there, offering shelter to the homeless. Half a dozen people gathered around a fire, a couple holding their hands out to the flames as the others rubbed them briskly to get their blood circulating. Others, away from the fire, crawled inside their cardboard homes in search of some protection from the elements. Every time one of them moved he felt his heart skip a beat. Each movement caused him to tense his muscles. With every sound he was sure he'd been found, but it was like he didn't exist to them. Even when Sasha eventually returned he didn't move. He listened to her walk beneath the archways as she entered the outsiders' sanctuary, calling out his name. He needed to be sure it was really her.

'I'm here,' he said at last, scrambling down the banked paving stones.

'We have to do this quickly,' Sasha said as he reached her.

'Where is he?'

'Who?'

'The man who's going to burn the chip?'

She smiled. It was a surprisingly mischievous smile.

Sasha turned and beckoned to someone out of sight.

Cal edged his way forward, his feet scuffing on the concrete as he slid down the slope from his hiding place. He wanted to get a better look at who she was waving to. He saw someone else standing in the mouth of the archways. The figure was slight with a hood pulled up over his head. He didn't move until

Sasha summoned him, and even then he approached with great care. Cal could sense his nervousness. Sasha said nothing more until he reached them.

Cal studied the newcomer. He wore tight jeans, battered high-top trainers and a heavy green parka that engulfed his frame. He didn't look like a saviour. Actually, he looked like a kid who'd stolen an adult's clothes to play dress-up.

'Who's this?' Cal asked.

'Danni,' Sasha said. 'Danni's going to sort your chip out.'

'Pleased to meet you,' Danni said, thrusting out a hand and pulling the hood back at the same time.

'You're . . .' Cal started to stay, not sure how he could end the sentence without offending his would-be saviour.

'A girl?' she said as her hair fell back from her face. 'Yes, I know. Have been my entire life.'

'That wasn't what I was going to say,' Cal lied badly.

'Yes it was.' She grinned at him, enjoying his discomfort. 'But that's fine. It's a statement of fact, not an accusation, right? It's not like you'd think less of me because I'm a girl or anything, is it?'

He nodded, wishing the ground would open up beneath his feet and swallow him. 'I'm sorry . . . I didn't mean . . . It's just . . .'

'Yep, all of that. And I'll forgive you, just this once, but don't go making a habit of it, eh?'

Cal looked at Danni. She was no older than he was. Pretty, in a punky kind of way, shorter than him by a good twenty centimetres, with shocking blue hair that blazed her personality loud and clear. She didn't look like a trained physician, yet she wanted to go rooting around in his head, messing with his chip and the interface where it anchored to his brain? There was absolutely no way he was about to let her probe around inside his head. This was crazy. There had to be someone else who could do this? A proper doctor. What if she screwed up and fried his brain?

Sasha read his mind. 'She's done loads of these,' she said, knowing he needed the reassurance. 'Just focus on me.'

Just focus on her? That was like asking him to let a stranger poke inside his skull with a burning wire – actually it wasn't *like* that at all. It was exactly that. And it wasn't going to happen.

Sasha took hold of his hands, squeezing them tight, but Cal could not take his eyes off Danni.

She reached into her pocket and pulled out a device with two metal prongs, like a Taser. The contraption was bound together with electrical tape. It looked horribly home-made and potentially lethal.

Cal pulled away suddenly, slipping out of Sasha's grasp. He tried to think, but it was hopeless. Where could he run? Back under the bridge, up in the cracks where he'd been hiding only a few minutes before? Home? To the doors of the Watchhouse back in the plaza to throw himself on Marshall Trent's mercy? He was a reasonable man, wasn't he? He cared for them. He only wanted what was best for all his people? Cal stumbled away a couple of steps, trying to go back up the bank as if he could disappear beneath the arches while the world went on trip-trapping over his head. But his heel slid and he completely lost his footing.

Instinctively he reached out for something to cling on to, realising the river was only metres away down a sharp embankment to his left.

The noise brought up a curious head from within the depths of the cardboard city, but seeing the kids it went down again, either disinterested or through self-preservation.

Cal's hand slapped at a concrete pillar, but he couldn't get any kind of grip with his fingers, and he was falling properly now, and there was nothing he could do to stop himself plunging into the water. The baseball cap slipped from his head as he was pulled under by the current, then he bobbed back to the surface, coughing.

The cap was already ten metres away and being carried further away by the river.

There was nothing between his Neurochip and the Enforcers hunting him.

He splashed and twisted, trying to swim after it, but couldn't reach it. The slow-moving water stank of decay and yet weeds were thriving in the effluence. Cal swallowed a mouthful as he tried to scramble back up the sheer bank and hang on to the bag with the precious fruit at the same time. He gagged at the foul taste, but the slow current was dragging him downstream as he fought it. He cried out for help as he went under again, swallowing huge mouthfuls of the foul water and then hands closed round his flailing arms and pulled him out.

The girls dragged him back to dry land, scraping his belly and thighs on the concrete.

Cal spluttered and tried to get to his feet.

Then he saw his bag slowly sinking and stooped to retrieve it, only for one of the girls to yell, 'Get back under the bridge, you idiot!' He couldn't tell who. He couldn't stop coughing as they hauled him back into the shadows.

'We don't have any time to lose,' Danni said.

He couldn't fight her. Cal felt fingers pushing his hair back, exploring the bump beneath the skin behind his ear. He tried to pull away, but the girls pinned him down. No matter how much he struggled, he couldn't get them off.

'Keep still,' Sasha demanded.

He felt a sudden sting as the device released an electric charge into the Neurochip. He could smell his own burning skin. Danni sprayed something on his neck, which relieved the searing pain and then the girls released their grip on him. It was over. They'd burned his chip out. He was one of them now.

'We've got to get out of here quickly,' Sasha urged, getting to her feet.

Cal spat the last traces of foul-tasting water from his mouth. He sat up. He felt sick, tired and frightened.

'What's the hurry? You've killed this thing; they can't find us now.' He gingerly brought a finger to the skin behind his ear, desperately wanting to touch it but frightened of the hurt it might bring.

'Because the moment you lost the hat they could see you,' Sasha said. 'Because that changes everything. If they know where we are, we have to be somewhere else. And because we have to meet someone.'

'Who?' Cal demanded. He glanced down at the mess he'd made of his clothes and then back at the water where his bag and its contents had disappeared beneath the surface. He shook his head. 'I should have just let them catch you,' he said, shaking his head. But he didn't mean it, even if they had burned the chip out of his head.

'Buccaneer,' Sasha said, ignoring him.

'As in the leader of the Anarchists? We're going to meet the leader of the Anarchists? The most wanted criminal in the country? *That* Buccaneer?'

'Is there another?'

'Honestly? I hope so. I hope there's a nice friendly Buccaneer who visits sick kids in the hospital and hands out sweets to kids doing Penny for the Guy.'

'Well, Buccaneer and Guy Fawkes certainly have something in common,' Danni said, flashing him a dangerous grin. 'The whole burning-down-Parliament thing. You got that, right? Anyway, folks, I'm out of here,' said Danni, stowing her things in her coat's deep pockets. 'Pleasure to meet you, Cal. Good luck with the rest of your life. Who knows, we might even meet again if you're a good boy.'

'You're not coming with us?' Cal asked.

'Not me,' she said. 'I'm needed somewhere else.' She patted her pockets as if to say that it was her expertise that was required, that there were others who wanted to have their lives irreversibly changed.

Maybe Cal wasn't alone. Maybe he had become part of something that was growing. It might not have been his choice, but that didn't mean it wasn't theirs. He thought about the images of the burning outpost in Bright Town, and how it could have been any building, anywhere. And he thought about the dead boy with the bloody wound where his chip had been burned out. Was that what was going to happen to him?

He hadn't asked for any of this. He wasn't an Anarchist. He believed in everything Marshall Trent had done for them. All Trent wanted to do was rebuild the world. Where was the crime in that?

Danni nodded, then pulled her hood back up over her bright blue cropped hair, and disappeared through the archways, picking a path through the cardboard boxes and the outsiders huddled around their braziers, and was gone, back out into the light.

'What now?' Cal asked.

'Now we go and meet Buccaneer,' Sasha said and started to walk back the way they'd come, confident that their precautions would mean no one was waiting for them.

She was wrong.

Three Enforcers hid, metallic claws digging deep into the stone wall above the mouth of the archways, just out of sight. The Enforcers pushed away from the wall and dropped down on Cal and Sasha from above as they stepped out of the cardboard city. Shockwaves rumbled through the ground as they landed, pistons and servos absorbing the incredible impact.

Cal turned to run, but before he could manage a single step the searing sting of a stun baton turned his world black.

Chapter 5

'You awake?'

Cal heard the voice coming through the dull thud that filled his head. It took him a moment to realise it was Sasha's. He tried to open his eyes and sit up, but a wave of nausea hit him hard, convincing him it was a bad idea. Instead he lay still while his senses came slowly back. The best he could manage was to let out a groan, but at least she'd know he was alive.

From somewhere deep in the distance he heard the distinctive heavy sounds of an Enforcer moving closer.

'Quick,' Sasha said, urging him up.

He didn't want to move, but sat up anyway, his head still spinning. Pain throbbed behind his eyes. The room they were in was less like a cell and more like a waiting room, but given how they'd got here it was unlikely they'd enjoy this luxury for much longer.

'You OK?' he asked, his fingers feeling the sore patch behind his ear. He winced at the contact.

'Yeah. At least Danni got away,' she said.

Cal gave a grunt of disbelief. 'You think? Don't you find it the least bit strange there were three of them waiting for us and that somehow she managed to slip away?'

24

'She's good at what she does.'

'Or maybe she isn't.'

'What are you trying to say?'

Cal wasn't exactly trying to hide what he was thinking. There was no way Danni should have been able to give the Enforcers the slip, even if they didn't have her Neurochip's PID to guide them. She'd given them the all-clear and they'd walked out into an ambush. There was only one reasonable explanation. She'd sold them out. But why? Was she one of them?

'She wouldn't betray us. She's vital to the cause, one of Buccaneer's most trusted hackers; she's brilliant, not a traitor,' Sasha said. Cal didn't contradict her, but wanted to point out the irony of arguing that someone who was an Anarchist wasn't a traitor just because they chose to call themselves a freedom fighter.

'What did you do with my rig?'

'Don't worry I got rid of it.'

'How?'

'I slipped it down through one of the sewer grates. It amuses me to think of the Enforcers wading through everyone's waste trying to find you.'

'It's probably on its way out to sea now,' Cal said, suddenly remembering the foul taste of the river water, realising exactly what was flushed into the water from all over the city.

'It could be halfway to France by now.'

'Shame we're not,' Cal said, just to say something rather than leave them in an awkward silence. 'Any idea where we are?' he asked, looking around. It was an utterly unremarkable place. Pale grey walls. Functional furniture. No flowers or ornaments apart from a large picture of Marshall Trent that looked down at them.

'You were lucky this time,' the picture of Marshall Trent said.

It wasn't a picture, Cal realised, looking at it properly for the first time. It was a display screen.

'Lucky?' Cal whispered to Sasha. 'Why would he think we were lucky? If we had been lucky, we would still be out there.'

'Shhh,' Sasha said, not taking her eyes off the screen.

'You were lucky because I was looking out for you, Sasha. I want to keep you safe, but I can't. Not if you insist on this rebellion. This has to stop.'

How does he know her name? Cal wondered. *And why would he be looking out for her?* Cal's mind was racing. She was one of the Anarchists that Trent had been warning everyone about, but he was talking about protecting her? It didn't make sense.

'I don't need *keeping safe*,' she said, deliberately mimicking him.

'Oh, I think you do, Sasha. You are mixing with some very dangerous people. Deviants. They want to tear the world apart for fun. They don't *want* anything. They don't offer any answers. They aren't romantic heroes. They aren't freedom fighters. They are terrorists. They might argue those are different words to describe the same thing, but they really aren't. They offer nothing good to this country. All I do, I do for the best of my people. You know that. And when you are out there with them, it's not easy for the Enforcers to distinguish between those intent on damaging our proud nation, and those who are just misguided and easily led.' Trent's gaze drifted down to Cal. 'Which group do you belong to, Callaghan?

Cal tried to find the words to answer, to explain that none of this was his doing, he'd only tried to stop the girl from being hurt, but under the intense stare of the great moving head on the wall he couldn't find the words. Marshall Trent knew his name. Marshall Trent knew everything there was to know about him. That was how it worked. He would know where he lived. And that meant he knew where his father lived. Without thinking, Cal again reached up to touch the wound where his chip had been. Destroying it hadn't made anything better. It hadn't saved them or stopped Trent's Enforcers finding him. It had only made everything *worse*.

'Don't blame Cal,' Sasha said, cutting across him before he could find an excuse that might have sounded believable. 'He was just trying to help me. I would be dead if it wasn't for him.'

'An innocent victim *and* a hero? Well, aren't you the busy boy, Callaghan.' Cal didn't say anything. 'But that doesn't explain why your chip has been destroyed, does it? That would suggest you are anything but innocent. Unless what happened was against your will? Is that it, Callaghan?'

Trent was giving him a way out, or seemed to be. So why did it feel like a trap? If he told the man what had happened, how Danni had burned his chip out while Sasha held him down, it might buy his freedom, but at what cost to Sasha? He couldn't betray her. She hadn't set out to ruin his life. Trent clearly knew her, though, and cared enough to want to keep her safe. Cal needed time to think, because he couldn't come up with an answer that didn't sound pathetic, so he said nothing.

'How did you find us?' Sasha asked, buying him a few precious seconds.

'I have my ways, girl.' He turned his attention back to Cal. 'I suppose I should be grateful to you for saving Sasha.' Still, Cal said nothing. 'And ultimately for leading me to her. Oh, you didn't know?'

'It was when I fell into the river,' Cal said, breaking his silence. 'The Enforcers picked up the signal from my chip before . . . it . . . malfunctioned,' he said.

'Not bad, Callaghan. You are clearly brighter than you look,' Marshall Trent said, with the hint of a smile at the edges of his mouth.

'What are you going to do to him?' Sasha asked. It was the same question that was bouncing around inside Cal's head.

'Do to him? You make me sound like a barbarian, girl. I won't *do* anything to him. It's not his fault that he tried to be chivalrous without considering the consequences of his actions. It's not his fault that the Enforcers didn't manage to get you off the street sooner. It's not his fault that he ended up damaging his Neurochip. He will learn a valuable lesson from this, though. Isn't that right, Cal?'

Sasha answered for him, widening the smile on Trent's face. 'That's right. He's done nothing wrong. It's my fault. I tricked him into thinking he had to run. I used him to help me escape. I made him think he was putting other people's lives in danger. He's loyal to you.' She turned to Cal. 'Aren't you, Cal? You're loyal to Marshall Trent?'

Cal couldn't believe that she was talking to Marshall Trent like this. Bargaining with him. Treating him like an equal. Then it dawned on him: this wasn't just a case of Trent knowing their names, Trent knew Sasha and she knew him.

Trent paused for a moment, glancing from one to the other then back again. 'Never let it be said I am unfair. I believe in offering good people second chances. There's little to be gained from putting you to work in the mines or the steel works that are so desperately needed to rebuild this country, Cal. You have a bright future ahead of you. Or you did, until today. It will be better for society if you accept that you have made a mistake and return to your family. But I need your assurance that you will keep your head down, stay away from Buccaneer and these New Luddites who are so intent on destroying everything I have worked hard to achieve. They aren't good people, Cal. Believe me. All I want is for you to be a model Citizen. Can you do that for me, Cal?'

'Yes, of course.' He was ready to accept almost any condition if it meant he could walk out of there and back into his normal life. He didn't want to have anything to do with the Anarchists. All he wanted to do was go home.

'I'm so glad to hear that, Cal. I will arrange for you to have your damaged Neurochip replaced with a functioning one before you leave, but do not let anyone tamper with this one. We will know. And while I give second chances, I won't give third ones. I'm not that kind of man. If anything happens to your chip, you will be treated as a traitor and so will the rest of your family. Do I make myself clear?'

'Y-yes, sir,' he stuttered, not quite believing he was getting off so lightly.

Sasha had been involved in the explosion that had taken out a Watchhouse. That was an open act of terrorism. He'd saved her life, and for all Marshall Trent knew had been a key part in her escape plan, and yet he was going to be allowed to walk away?

It didn't feel right.

This wasn't the Marshall Trent from the news streams who promised no quarter for the enemy. Something was wrong, and as much as he didn't want to jeopardise his freedom, Cal couldn't help himself. He asked, 'What's going on, Sasha?'

The girl's cheeks turned red, flushed with embarrassment, but it was Marshall Trent who answered his question. 'She hasn't told you who she is then?'

'We only met –' Cal stopped when he realised he had no idea how much time had passed since the clock had struck thirteen and his life had changed. How long had they been unconscious? Was this even the same day? He had to get home before his father started worrying about him.

Trent enjoyed his confusion, making a show of checking an antiquated fob watch on an old gold chain. 'You met less than five hours ago,' he said.

Only five hours?

'So, will you tell him, dear girl, or shall I?'

There was a secret between the two of them and he wanted to know what it was.

Sasha turned to him, her face now red with anger not embarrassment. 'Marshall Trent is my father.'

Chapter 6

The houses were in near darkness. Thin clouds scudded across the moon. It was a starless sky.

It had been a long time since the electric lights had last worked in the streets around Cal's home. In the Communities where the rich and privileged lived it was different; the lights still blazed there, but not here. Here, people slaved away simply to survive. They didn't have many luxuries, and those they did they certainly didn't waste by burning them all night long in the middle of the street. These houses were all the same, row after row of tiny two-storey buildings crammed together, built in factories and assembled on shallow foundations. There was nothing permanent about them. They'd been thrown together quickly and cheaply to provide shelter for families displaced and made homeless in the Last Great Civil War, which had changed this country beyond all recognition. They were supposed to be temporary, built to last ten years, no more, but they had stood for more than fifty now, patched up again and again with no sign of anything more permanent replacing them. One day not too far away, the decay eating away at the high-tensile metal frames would go beyond any kind of patching and thousands upon thousands of people would be out on the streets.

A dog barked nearby and something moved in the road ahead of him. It scuttled in the darkness. Even without seeing it, Cal knew that it was a rat. He'd seen enough to know them by sound alone. They were a fact of life here. He picked up a stone and threw it in the general direction of the scratching sound, even though there was little chance of hitting it. The stone clattered along the broken road, adding to the debris scattered everywhere. No one cared enough to keep the place tidy, because that would mean accepting that their future lay among the ruins. Everyone here wanted to leave for a better life. They still had dreams.

Cal wasn't looking forward to explaining what had happened to his rig, or where he'd been all day. The loss of the rig was a blow. They couldn't afford a new one. Even a cheap replacement would be pushing it. But that wasn't what hurt. It had been his mother's. It was one of the few things of hers that he still had.

He wasn't sure what he was going to tell his dad. He was grateful he'd been allowed to walk away once the new chip had been inserted, rather than being escorted by Enforcers. Not that he would have been the first in the Community to have been brought home by the droids, but it would have started the ragged curtains twitching and tongues flapping. No smoke without fire, that was what they said, wasn't it?

Cal walked on.

To strangers every house looked the same, every street corner identical. There were no street signs any more. They'd been stripped and sold as scrap metal decades ago. When he'd been younger they had tricked strangers by giving them directions the long way round, and then taken shortcuts to appear on another street corner, leaving the visitors thinking they'd come full circle.

Although he had spent most of his time in the heart of New Edgehill, these four walls were still the place that meant most to him. It was the only home he'd ever known. Once upon a time, back before his mother died, they'd lived in a much bigger and better house on the other side of the city. But afterwards his father had not wanted to go back to it. So they lived here. That wasn't the only thing his father didn't want to do. He never wanted to talk about his mother, even when Cal asked what she was like because he couldn't remember her any more. All his dad would say was that life might have been different if she'd never gone away. Cal believed him, but only because that was the only truth he'd ever known. It was difficult. He was growing up. Changing. Forgetting more and more stuff. But there was no way of escaping the fact that this was the only life he could ever have lived. Anything else was just daydreaming – and his dad did a lot of that, sitting with a faraway look in his eyes, pretending he was in a happier place. Living in the past was dangerous because the present could never compete with it.

But every now and then Cal wished he was still that mischievous kid, that his mum was still alive and that everything that had happened to his family since she died was nothing but a bad dream. What he wouldn't give to not have a care in the world. But he did. He had the weight of the world on his young shoulders and this was home. Home didn't have to be four walls. Sometimes it was just a place in the world where you belonged, and this Community was where he belonged.

Cal didn't want a life of excitement; he wanted the ordinary, the normal. He wanted things to be the way they had always been.

Cal walked through the familiar streets lost in thought, not looking up until he reached the huge display screen that served their part of the Community. Even here the face of Marshall Trent was seen on a regular basis. These massive screens were the only things guaranteed to receive power, and, if something happened to them, they were the only pieces of equipment that would be repaired without delay. These screens were the government's mouthpieces, they talked directly to the Communities and kept people in line, as well as up to date with what was happening in the world. Most recently they'd been filled with pictures of the growing threat of war overseas and the dead Anarchist in front of the ruined Exploratory Outpost in Bright Town. These screens showed the people they mattered to Marshall Trent. They promised that, no matter how far away they were and how much they suffered, they were not forgotten. They were still important.

The crack in the house at the end of Seventy-Seventh Street looked like a black scar running from the ground to the roof. It had been patched up so many times that there were more black tar-paper squares than the original wall. But it was home.

Another dog barked in the distance, or maybe it was the same one. Few people kept a pet these days. It was hard enough feeding themselves without willingly taking on another mouth to feed. Somehow the animals always found food, even though half of them were little more than skin and bone.

From the corner of his eye he saw the big black infoscreen burst into life, filling the street with light as power surged through it.

It *never* broadcast this late at night. Never.

Which meant it had to be an emergency. Something that couldn't wait until the morning.

Three words lit up the screen. No image, no sign of Marshall Tent's face looming over him, just three simple words. *Open Your Eyes.* The message stayed there for a heartbeat and then disappeared, leaving a faint afterglow that slowly faded. The hum disappeared as quickly as it had appeared.

Cal was the only person in the street, meaning the message must have been meant for him. What could it possibly mean?

Chapter 7

Cal woke to the sound of someone moving in his room.

At first he thought it was his father coming in to check on him, so he had lain there pretending to be asleep, not moving so much as a muscle while trying to make his breathing sound loud and natural. He'd been expecting a row when he'd finally reached home, but instead his father had hugged him, kissed him and told him he was relieved Cal was home and safe. He was always the same; always more concerned about his safety than anything else. The discussion about responsibilities and what losing his rig meant, in terms of the sacrifices they'd have to make as a family to replace it, that would come over the next few days, but while they were both tired and a little emotional they hugged. Cal felt safe in his dad's arms. It was the only time he'd felt safe all day.

He opened one eye, expecting to see light streaming in through his open bedroom door, but there was nothing but darkness. The door itself looked to be firmly closed. There was, however, the slightest of drafts. The window was open, even though he knew he'd closed it before he'd crawled into bed.

He started to sit up, then caught sight of movement again as someone quickly closed the distance between the window and his bed.

He was about to cry out when a hand clamped over his mouth and pushed his head back down on to the pillow. Before he could react, a knee came up and pressed down on to his chest, pinning him on the bed.

He clawed at his assailant, trying to get himself free, but his attacker was stronger than him.

'Shhh,' the intruder whispered, a knee pressing even harder into Cal's ribs.

He fought against the pain, pushing in an attempt to free himself.

He heard the fizzle and spark of electricity, and saw a blue glow in the darkness.

'Danni?' he mumbled into the hand clamped over his mouth, thinking it was the girl's cropped hair he'd seen, but as he bucked again he saw it wasn't her.

Sasha. She looked terrifying looming over him in the dark. Terrifying *and* incredibly strong. Cal managed to reach across with his free hand and knocked the device from her grip. He wasn't about to let her burn his new Neurochip out, not after what Marshall Trent had threatened to do to him and his family. Cal broke free of her grip as she scrambled to retrieve it.

He reached up to turn on the reading light above his bed. 'What do you think you're doing?' he demanded, barely daring to whisper. He really didn't want his dad coming in to his room. He knew exactly what Sasha was trying to do, and she was trying to do it even though she knew exactly what the consequences would be.

'I'm setting you free, that's what I'm doing.'

He shook his head. 'Are you crazy? Don't you remember what your father said? It's not just me you're putting at risk, it's my dad, too.' And then without thinking he said, 'You may not love your father, but I love mine. He's all I've got. Don't do this to me, please.' Before she could answer, Cal went on, 'How did you even get here? Surely he's got you under lock and key after today?'

'Dear old daddy. I've spent most of my life dreaming up ways to escape from him. The problem is he still thinks he can change me. He doesn't learn. He thinks that he can give me another chance to prove that I can be trusted, and another one and another one. Every time I disappoint him he forgives me and gives me another chance to screw up. He says I am troubled. I call it free will.'

'But what about your chip?'

She laughed at that. 'I guess he's given up replacing mine now. After a dozen he stopped. I cut the first one out myself with a scalpel and a pair of tweezers. I clawed one out this morning with my fingernails.' She lifted up her hair to show him the scars.

'You did what?' He couldn't believe what she was saying. She had actually stuck a knife into her neck to get her chip out. How was that even possible? There was an interface back there, beneath the skin. It was sensitively aligned between nerve pathways and receptors, fused with the cerebral cortex – meaning it was hotwired right into her brain – at least when they burned it out they weren't rooting around trying to pry the chip and its relics out of the interface, they were just neutralising it, clawing it out could do so much damage. He shuddered at the thought.

'You haven't seen what I've seen, Cal,' she said, keeping her voice low. 'If you had, you'd feel exactly the same way about that monstrosity. You wouldn't want it in your head a moment longer. It goes two ways, that connection, Cal. They share data with you, but that's not the half of it. They can hear everything you say, hear everything you hear, see what you see. For all I know they can read every single thought you have. Everything that crosses your mind. You have no secrets. No privacy. They are watching and listening to everything you do or say. And now you're awake, they'll know I'm here. It's only a matter of time before they get here.'

'I'll tell them that you broke in.'

'And you think that they'll believe you? After what we've already been through? Once they realise I know where you live they'll find it hard to believe that you didn't know me *before* the explosion. And then they'll get suspicious and start to think that you really were involved in that.'

Cal shook his head. 'They can't do that. You know that isn't true.' Then he started to think, to use his brain for a second.

'If they're listening now, they'll know you're lying . . . you're confessing it to them right now. Just leave me alone, please,' he said. 'If you're not here, there's nothing they can do, nothing they can prove. You were never here. This whole thing was just a dream.'

'Proof doesn't come into it, Cal. You've got to come with me quickly, but I have to do something about your chip now.'

'No,' he snapped, his voice louder than he'd intended. He didn't want to wake his father, but perhaps he'd assume he'd heard raised voices from one of the houses nearby through the paper-thin walls, rather than Cal arguing with a mad girl who wanted to ruin his life.

'You've got to, Cal. If you don't, you'll never know the truth.'

'Maybe I don't want to know the truth. Maybe I'm happy the way things are. Maybe I want things to be back the way they were before I ever met you. Maybe I wish I'd let the Enforcer hit you instead of helping you escape.'

'You don't mean that,' she said, but she didn't sound certain. It was the first time he had heard any sort of vulnerability or doubt from the girl. Looking at her now, she finally seemed younger than him. He took a step towards her. 'You can't possibly want to go back to that. Not now that you've had a glimpse of what the world is really like.'

'Don't I? I don't care what the world's like. This is my home, this is my life, this is all I want. Come back in twenty years and ask me if I managed to forget all about you.'

'But this is important, Cal. I didn't realise who you were until a few hours ago. But now I know. You've got to come with me.'

'What are you talking about?'

'I can't tell you, Cal. Not here. Not while you've still got that chip in your head.'

'Then we've got a problem, because I'm not going anywhere until you tell me what this is all about.'

He couldn't admit it even to himself, but he was already thinking about going with her. He couldn't understand why. It wasn't the promise of adventure. It was more than that. He glanced at the pile of clothes on the chair near his bed and knew that it would only take a minute to slip into them again. Then he glanced at the window and knew they could be gone in less than two if he put his mind to it.

Sasha didn't reply. She cocked her head to one side, listening intently.

'What is it?'

'*Shhh!*'

From her expression it was obvious something was wrong. Even before she spoke again he was out of bed and pulling on his jeans and a jumper.

'It's a Drone,' she said. 'We *have* to get out of here, Cal. I need to neutralise your chip.'

She already had the device in her hand, the spark of electricity crackling between the two metal points as she held it up.

He shook his head. 'Not until you tell me what this is all about.' He closed the gap between them and reached out to take hold of her hands. He wasn't ready. She needed to understand that.

She held eye contact with him for a moment until he heard the steady hum of the Drone rapidly approaching. They didn't have long to make their escape. Every second was precious. But she knew something that she wasn't telling him. He wasn't about to have Marshall Trent brand both him and his father traitors without knowing exactly why he was doing it.

'All right,' she said at last, giving in. 'It's about your mother.'

Chapter 8

Sasha pulled an old laptop computer from her rucksack. It was an antique, a relic of the Last Great Civil War. The technology behind it was basic, lacking any sort of uplink to the *Neuralnet*. Cal had never seen anything like it outside history class.

'Does it work?'

She nodded.

Cal reached behind his ear. The moment she'd mentioned his mother he'd known he was going to go with her, and that meant she'd have to disable his chip. He didn't want to think about what else it meant. It was enough to try to cope with one problem at a time, and the Drone that kept passing over the Community was a reminder that Marshall Trent could find him as long as the chip was active. Of course, right now, here was exactly where he was supposed to be, so any signal his chip broadcast back to the Watchhouses was OK. Not that it was a choice. He needed to know what she knew about his mother, what she'd meant when she'd said she hadn't realised who he was until a few hours ago. The only way he was going to get answers meant leaving with Sasha. Which meant killing the chip inside his head . . . again.

'It's not hooked up to the net, obviously, which means we can use it without *him* knowing what we're up to,' Sasha said. Him being her father, the man who had quelled the disturbances of the war and brought years of peace with his iron rule.

She held the laptop out to Cal. He took the machine from her and ran his hands across the surface. He felt for the catch that would release the screen.

'I've seen one like this before,' he said, realising it was true. 'Not just in school or some museum . . .' But he had no idea where. Maybe in some wrecker's yard when he was scavenging parts for his rig? Cal had fooled around with enough rigs and

devices over the years to have encountered the same basic
circuitry if not operating system. He felt around for something
to power it up, bringing the laptop humming to life.

'You know how to use it?'

'Not a clue. Mum used to use an old laptop like this.' He
was thinking fast. It wasn't organic or bio-dependent, like his
rig. There wasn't anything to suggest it was locked to a single
user by genetic code or anything as elaborate as that. 'It's got a
keyboard, so that's got to be a good place to start,' he said with
a grin. 'But this thing's old.'

'Is it even going to understand the kind of code we use?'
Sasha wondered. He'd been worrying about the exact same
thing. What if it spoke a dead language?

'Only one way to find out.'

He wouldn't know until he'd got deep into the OS.

The only thing he was reasonably sure of was that it
wouldn't be like using a rig; those were attuned to their thought
waves as much as anything else. Whereas, a machine like
this . . . it would be like needing to know an ancient language to
speak to it. Like Latin or Greek, or in this case machine code.

The fan stopped humming. Instead of the login screen he'd
expected the screen filled with letters, an endless cycling array of
ASCII scrolling across the screen. He couldn't tell if it was some
kind of code, or if there was a message hidden in plain sight.
He should have expected the machine to be protected. He hit
the escape key, the enter key, the space bar – nothing happened.
Thinking on his feet, Cal hit 'B' for Buccaneer and a symbol
slowly resolved amid the stream of letters: a simple circle over a
square, the symbol of the Anarchist Buccaneer.

He tried pressing a couple more keys, but this time nothing
happened. The square in the circle kept on rotating, the two
symbols interlocking.

Cal glanced up at Sasha. 'Any ideas?'

She'd moved back to his bedroom window and was keeping a lookout for the tell-tale shadows of Drones in the sky or Enforcers marching down the street.

'Nope,' she said, watching him through the reflection in the glass. 'You've got to crack it, Cal. We don't have all night. He'll have realised I've come back to you the moment he noticed I'm gone. The clock's ticking. And we're not moving. That means we're sitting ducks.'

'That's really not helpful,' he replied. He tried another combination of keys, running through words he thought might mean something to Buccaneer, like 'Luddite', 'New Luddite', 'pirate' and 'anarchy', but none of them had any effect on the image on the screen. 'But you're right. We can't stay here,' he said. 'It's taking too long.'

'A couple of minutes ago you wanted to send me on my way so you could pretend to be a good little boy and not get involved . . .'

'A couple of minutes ago you hadn't told me this was about my mother.'

He couldn't look at her as he said it. He stared at the circle and the square on the screen and felt the vague stirring of a memory deep down in a part of his brain that had lain dormant for years: a trick his mother had shown him on her old computer. It wasn't a hack, or a back door or anything like that, it was just an amusement he'd always assumed she made for him. She was good like that. Actually, come to think of it, the pattern of keys triggered a hidden line of code and rabbits reproduced across the screen – first one, then a second, then two more, three more, five more, eight, thirteen, twenty-one, filling the screen. Fibonacci's rabbits. There was a mathematical code behind the sequence. He knew it. Learning it was the last happy memory he had of his mother. Without thinking about what he was doing, he tested his memory to see if this old laptop would dance to the same tune. He entered Fibonacci's sequence of numbers, one for each month of the year, counting the rabbits in his mind – 0, 1, 1, 2, 3, 5, 8, 13, 21, 34, 55, 89, 144 – and waited to see what would happen.

His heart skipped a beat as the screen changed, the circle and square disappearing. This was a message for him and him alone. It was too much of a coincidence to think that anyone could have stumbled upon that number sequence by accident. This time it wasn't a procession of rabbits multiplying on his screen. A line of text moved across the monitor. It wasn't repeated. But he didn't need to see it twice.

Get out of there quickly, Cal. It's not safe.

A second line followed the first.

Go. Now. Run!

'Everything OK?' Sasha asked.

He shook his head. 'No. Not at all.'

There was a webcam lens in the centre of the laptop lid, but the indicator was off. They couldn't have been watching him. Sasha had said there was no uplink on the old machine. He tried to think. He closed the laptop, still shaking his head.

Whoever had sent the message had known about the trick with Fibonacci's rabbits his mother had shown him, but maybe it wasn't rare back then? Maybe everyone knew about it?

'Who gave you this?' he asked.

'Buccaneer. I was told to get it to you. That it was important. That it was about your mother and that you'd know what to do.'

And he had, hadn't he? But how could Buccaneer have possibly known how to get past the security? And how could that message have been pre-programmed? Unless it was just meant to scare him?

He had a choice to make. A big one. He either had to trust the machine and get out of there, or not. He didn't give himself time to think about it. 'We've got to move,' he said.

'Are you ready?' she asked, throwing the open rucksack to him.

He stuffed the laptop inside, then pushed the hair back away from his neck and leaned forward. 'I really hope you know what you are doing.'

She didn't answer. The slightest slip could do irreversible damage to his brain. He couldn't get the image of the dead Anarchist boy out of his mind. But he trusted her. He trusted her as much as he had ever trusted anyone in his life. He chewed on his lower lip as he heard the familiar fizz of electricity, and waited for the burn.

The sudden jolt of pain made him cry out. She clamped a hand over his mouth. All he could smell for the next minute or more was the faint tang of burning flesh.

'You OK?' Sasha asked when she finally took her hand away.

'Been better,' he said. 'How many of these have you done?' he asked, rubbing at his neck.

'You were my first.'

'I'm really glad you didn't tell me that before you did it.'

She grinned. 'I've watched Danni do it enough times. Now, come on, let's get out of here.' She didn't wait for him to answer. She was already climbing through the window.

Cal slung the bag over his shoulder and followed her out into the night, casting one last lingering look back at his room, thinking about everything he was leaving behind. He almost didn't go. He almost turned back, half in and half out of the window, unwilling to turn his back on his dad, but Sasha urged him on, and he followed her.

Something had changed between them, he realised. He liked her. He trusted her. They'd become friends.

Scrambling down drainpipes with the bag heavy on his back wasn't easy, and it wasn't quiet, either. He kept looking over his shoulder at all the windows in the street, willing them to stay dark. The last thing he wanted was for one of the neighbours to see him creeping out of his bedroom window.

Sasha dropped to the ground, dusted her hands off on her knees and took off at a dash before he was even halfway down.

Cal had to sprint to keep up. She was fast. And, surprisingly, she seemed to know where she was going despite the streets all looking identical in the dark. She darted between housing blocks, dipping in and out of alleyways and shortcuts as if she'd lived there all her life. She knew her way through his Community as well as he did.

He had no idea where she was taking him. He'd expected her to try to leave the Community as quickly as possible, putting as much distance between them and his home as she could, but she obviously had somewhere in mind because instead of making for the outskirts and the roads that would take them to the next Community, closer to the rebuilt heart of New Edgehill, she wound her way through the back alleys, running deeper and deeper into the maze of buildings.

Giving him no warning, she dived into an alleyway between two run-down buildings and stopped dead in her tracks. She grabbed hold of him, throwing him up against the wall so hard it knocked the wind out of him. He was breathing hard. Again he was struck by her surprising strength. She might look like some elfin little girl, but she was as strong as an ox. Sasha clamped a hand over his mouth again, keeping him silent. He didn't fight her this time. The blood pounding through his head was only thing he could hear. No, there was something else . . . low and steady, the dull hum of an aerial surveillance Drone.

It was close. He listened as it drew nearer, waiting for it to appear in the open air between the buildings and see them, but the sound slowly receded.

'It's circling,' Sasha said. 'It hasn't got a fix on us yet, it's on a grid search eliminating the streets one by one. It'll be back soon.'

She was right, the silences between the Drone's presence in the sky above them grew shorter and shorter as it honed in on their whereabouts. It might not have the signal from his Neurochip to go on, but it could still track their heat sources and pick up movement.

And then she was running again.

'Where are we going?' he asked, trying to keep up with her.

'Somewhere safe,' she called back over her shoulder. 'Somewhere they won't find us.'

Cal ran after her. He had one plan in mind: stop when she stopped, run when she ran, and hide when she hid. That was it. If they were captured, she'd be safe – her father wouldn't let anything happen to her, but Cal would be on his own. There'd be no second chances, he knew that. So he ran. And he kept running until Sasha pulled aside a huge rusted iron door that looked as though it hadn't been opened in years.

'What's this?' he asked, gasping for breath.

He had absolutely no idea where they were.

'Sanctuary,' she said.

They were in a part of the Community that he rarely visited. Even so, he must have passed this door a thousand times without even noticing it was there.

Sasha closed the door behind them and led the way into darkness. As the door closed, emergency strip lights flickered on to reveal a flight of steps cut into what appeared to be bare rock. The passageway was narrow. They couldn't walk side by side. Then the lights failed. The only things they had to follow were the echoes of their footsteps in the cold dark space and the press of the walls around them.

Cal walked slowly, edging his way forward, trying to visualise the way in front of him, until he felt the emptiness of the first step drop away beneath him. He caught his balance before he fell, but, even so, the suddenness with which the ground dropped away was disorientating. He felt around the walls for handrails, and slowly descended one careful step at a time. The staircase wound round on itself and as it turned a faint glow of light appeared below them.

'I had no idea there was anything like this down here,' Cal said, marvelling at what he saw

'These are the remains of before.'

'Before?'

'Before my father came to power. Before the Community was built. Before the war. Before everything changed. I'm sure that the laptop will answer all your questions.'

Chapter 9

They retreated to a room that might have been a bomb shelter once upon a time. It was stripped to the bare essentials for survival, with a wire-framed bed and a metal table in the middle of the room, and a set of metal shelves that were stocked with long-life canned food that must have expired decades ago.

Cal put the bag on the table.

'We're safe here,' Sasha assured him, but he didn't feel safe.

48

'We're thirty metres underground,' she continued, 'the walls are lead-lined, the concrete foundations block out the Drones' heat tracers. They're blind. They can't see us, or hear us. Nothing we do down here can be monitored.'

'Are you sure?'

'Absolutely. Buccaneer has got half a dozen safe houses like this across New Edgehill, and more like them in every city. They are all off the grid. You can power up the laptop here. No one can spy on us.'

Cal took the relic from the backpack and set it down in the middle of the table. There was no charger in the bag, so he only had as long as the charge held to glean what he could from the machine, then he was on his own. He powered it up again. Again he was confronted by the ASCII-compiled streaming text that resolved into Buccaneer's circle and square icon. He tried the five-key trick again, expecting the laptop to surrender all its secrets to him, but it didn't.

The stream of ASCII characters returned, pouring down the screen in a seemingly endless cascade.

He tried the trick again, thinking he must have hit a wrong key.

'It's tied to your PID,' Sasha said.

That didn't help him.

'Surely you know how to extract your PID from your Neurochip?' This time she sounded incredulous.

He shook his head dumbly. 'You mean the one we just burned out?'

'Weren't you ever curious to know exactly what they had on you? It's the first thing I did when I realised the interface was two-way. I didn't trust my father with all my secrets. How could you not have hacked it?'

'Because until a few hours ago I was an ordinary law-abiding seventeen-year-old,' Cal protested. 'Why would I want to hack my PID? I didn't have anything to hide!'

'How could you *let* me burn it out?'

'I didn't have much of a choice,' he objected.

'What are we going to do?' Sasha said.

'Now you're worrying about that? A bit late, isn't it?'

'We need to get into the files on the laptop. They're keyed to you. Let me look at your neck. See if I can salvage something.'

Cal leaned forward, letting Sasha look at the wound where she'd used the Taser to burn out his Neurochip. Judging by the sounds she kept making there wasn't a lot of it left. Not enough to glean his PID from anyway. She cursed herself for a fool, then started rummaging around in her pockets until she found what she was looking for: a leather wrist brace. She strapped it on, and then peeled away one of several straps on it, revealing the inner mechanism of her own rig. It was far more sophisticated than Cal's had been, and much newer, but it lacked all the home-made mods he'd done to his own.

'I've got no idea if this'll work,' she admitted, teasing a silver-tipped monofilament wire from the casing and feeding it into the open wound in his neck. For a moment Cal thought it might have been a tiny camera, but it wasn't. The silver tip sank into the interface where some of the fragments of his ruined Neurochip had charred and fallen away, giving it access to *him*. 'Now this *is* going to hurt,' she said, making no apologies for what she was about to put him through. Using her rig she hacked her way through the layers of security that surrounded his own neural interface until she'd gone deep enough to pull up the schematics on her rig and could read him his own Personal Identifier that marked his entry point to the *Neuralnet*. It was even more uniquely him than his name. This was Callaghan Jones. The one and only.

Sasha knew her way around this stuff better than he did.

Cal entered the sequence, 2DADRQGVTDFYDQDIE, into the laptop and this time the old relic came to life, offering up its secrets, one nested folder at a time, starting with the first, which was simply labelled 'CAL'.

The images on the laptop were *nothing* like the broadcasts he'd seen on the super screens all across the city. He'd seen the aftermath of terrorist attacks, of the senseless devastation caused by factions like Buccaneer's New Luddites, and very real tragedies of violence and what it meant to rise against Marshall Trent's peace. But those images had always shown atrocities carried out by the enemy. Never by the forces of Marshall Trent. They only ever showed the brave and heroic efforts of our boys fighting to uphold the peace. This was different.

Each file showed Cal images that challenged everything he thought he knew about the world. These were images he simply couldn't *unsee*, no matter how desperately he wanted to. He thought again of the smoking ruin of the Exploratory Outpost in Bright Town and how it could have been any building, in any town, in any part of the world, and he would never have known any better because it was void of any recognisable features.

He looked at the images again.

Open Your Eyes. The words flashed across the screen.

The next layer of folders contained movie footage. Cal ran it and watched as the screen showed their own troops slaughtering innocents.

And there was no mistaking that was exactly what was happening. He watched as a platoon bearing the sigil of Marshall Trent ambushed a van, strafing it with a deadly rain of bullets. No one would be getting out of there alive. And then, worst of all, he watched the soldiers drag bodies out of the van, and when one moved, refusing to give up on life, he watched as an Enforcer swooped forward to stamp the life out of it.

That was where this footage had come from, Cal realised. It was from an Enforcer's on-board recorders. It was horrific. It was brutal and fast. Cal tried to rationalise it: surely these people were terrorists about to carry out some atrocity, some bombing, and the soldiers had just saved countless lives? But that wasn't what was happening. He knew that. As though to confirm his supposition, menus came up on the screen, reporting life signs, possible threats and confirmed that none of the hostiles were armed. Nor did any wear the uniforms of fighters in any conflict.

People needed to see these images. They needed to know the horrors that were being perpetrated in the name of peace, because it wasn't peace at all. They needed to . . . to what? Rise up?

Cal didn't know what he was supposed to do. He was just one young man, who until a few hours ago had been as blind as everyone else in Marshall Trent's paradise.

'What am I supposed to do with this?' he asked the computer.

'Information needs to be free.'

He didn't realise for a second that he hadn't imagined the voice, but rather that it came from the old laptop. It was a woman's voice.

The words had a dual meaning, too. Information shouldn't be withheld for a price, and neither should it be held prisoner. Information – in this case the truth – needed to be set free, because war wasn't supposed to be like this. War was about freedom not revenge. It was a last resort. How many times had Marshall Trent promised them he cared about the lives of every one of his soldiers? How many times had he sworn that he would do everything in his power to uphold the peace because all life was precious?

The pictures began to change too quickly for him to keep up with, though occasionally they paused for a second, letting the shocking images burn into his memory.

Then the images stopped showing soldiers fighting soldiers. There were no more Enforcers on the streets, now the view was

from aerial Drones and he was seeing bombs being dropped
on civilians. The next image was of children running with their
clothes on fire.

Cal felt sick. He wanted to look away but couldn't. It was
important that he watched everything. And, of course, there was
the possibility that these were lies meant to destroy his faith
in Marshall Trent and his peace. Buccaneer was Trent's enemy,
after all. Just because he traded in information and fashioned
himself a pirate of the new world didn't mean he was noble
or decent.

'Don't fall into the trap of believing everything you've been
told, Cal,' the voiceover said. There was no more death on the
screen; now the images showed the aftermath of war, revealing
what had survived. He had seen pictures like this before. The
pictures captured the ruins of the country as they had been at
the end of the Last Great Civil War. Some had now been rebuilt,
like New Edgehill and Bright Town, but many more hadn't.
'Is this what you thought it was like out there, Cal? No? What
about before the war? What have you been told about that?'

Cal wondered if he was supposed to answer. 'Is this
Buccaneer?' he asked as more images flashed in front of him,
speaking to Sasha.

'No,' Sasha said, but no more than that.

'Let's go back to the beginning,' the voice said as the screen
revealed a city street that looked like any street in the world
should have looked, with people moving happily from shop to
shop, heavily laden with bags and parcels. These people were
happy. This was the world before. Slowly the pictures changed.
Snow began to fall.

'This was the beginning of the global energy crisis. If you
believe the propaganda, we lost the supply of gas from Eastern
Europe and oil from the Middle East because our enemies cut
them off in order to bring this country to its knees. That is not

the truth. That was a story designed with one purpose: to create an enemy, because we needed someone to blame.'

Like everyone else, Cal had always been told that the energy crisis was why the Last Great Civil War had started, the tired, the cold and the hungry rising up against the government because of the shortages – shortages that had begun because other countries had refused to sell them what they needed. The riots followed because there wasn't enough to go around.

Snow fell on rooftops.

There were no people out on the streets.

The Big Freeze, they'd called it. He'd heard about that, too. It was the cold that had made the shortages worse.

'For years the government had encouraged people to use gas and electricity instead of burning wood and coal. It was supposed to be cleaner and cause less damage to the planet, but it meant that houses were no longer equipped to keep themselves warm using the resources all around them. The only power in the country was found in those areas that had been considered too remote to be worth the cost of installing mains gas, where they'd either installed subsidised solar panels or clung on to their open fires and wood-burning stoves. They stayed warm while the city dwellers went cold. Cold and hungry. It was bitterly different to the world they'd known, where they horded the wealth and power, where they were the haves and the poor, the have nots. Their world was suddenly upside-down.'

Cal could already see where this was going. He'd always been told that the war had been between the rich and the poor, and that the poor had risen up against the government to claim the country back for themselves. But looking at this, realising how history had subtly been rewritten, he could see that that wasn't how it was at all. As it unfolded on screen, he saw violence spread from the cities to what remained of the countryside, bled dry of natural resources and vitality. He saw crops being devastated by looters and livestock being fought over by men desperate to feed their families.

'There should have been enough food for everyone. It's a big world, with seemingly infinite resources. But we had relied too much on refrigerated and frozen imports instead of cooking fresh produce locally sourced from farms. When the power failed it was wasted. Spoiled. Those frozen dinners and processed meals went just as rotten as the freshest food. We were a bankrupt country, morally and financially. No one wanted to do business with us. Instead of trying to put things right, you saw what happened: the military killed indiscriminately, each group believing the other was responsible. This was no civil war, great or otherwise, this was the government against the rest of us, while those who could afford to fled. Finally the population came down to a point where we had enough resources to feed everyone. But by then it was too late.'

The screen showed millions of dead fish washed up on the beach, birds falling from the sky, dead before they hit the ground, and crops failing in the fields. Just when it looked as if the country had started to turn a corner, nature had given it another slap in the face. There was still an obvious tension in the images on the screen, but starvation was an enemy that people had in common.

'While the country was on its knees, a new way of magnifying and harnessing the sun's rays to create power was discovered, and it was the key to everything. With it, they were able to rebuild. Not everything. But they could make a start. It didn't have to be the end of the world. So much had been lost though, so much that could never be recovered. There were technologies that no longer worked and would need to be replaced somehow. There were cities that needed to rise up from the dust and debris, the rebuilding of which only served to make the rich richer while the surviving population struggled to feed themselves. But always one man kept control, pulling the strings at first, before stepping into the spotlight and being declared our saviour.'

Marshall Trent, thought Cal. But why had the government lied to them? Why had Marshall Trent made broadcasts to show how bad it was in the rest of the world?

'*Open Your Eyes, Cal,*' the voice said again.

The monitor showed the footage he had seen earlier that day on the infoscreen, the explosion and the close-up of a dead terrorist, the camera focussing on the scar behind his ear. Then, as the camera started to draw back, it revealed the whole of the scene, pulling further and further back to show the scope of the devastation, but it kept moving, revealing more than the news clips had ever shown. It showed the truth: what he'd just watched wasn't real. It was a film set.

'Sasha? I don't understand . . . how can it be true? How can he lie to us like that?' he asked. He looked at her beside him, seeing the same look of confusion on her face, but before she had the chance to respond his whole world was rocked by the deafening sound of an explosion.

Chapter 10

They moved back up to street level, abandoning the safe house before it could collapse around them.

The air up there was hot and full of dust and smoke.

Cal choked and gagged on it, holding his sleeve in front of his mouth to try to keep the worst of it at bay. In the immediate aftermath of the explosion all he could hear was a roaring sound that filled his ears, but eventually screams and cries and other noises began to filter through. They emerged back on the surface to see men, women and children running desperately through the streets, fleeing the source of the blast. There were others, braver souls, who pulled the injured from the rubble.

He felt lost.

'Cal!'

He heard his name being called again and again, but it took a moment to realise that Sasha was tugging at his sleeve and urging him to follow the throng of humanity as it flooded out of the Community, anxious to get away.

As far as he could see plumes of black smoke rose into the night sky. In the distance the red glow of burning buildings lit up the bruise purple horizon. The damage was everywhere. The wind was spreading the flames.

'We have to get out of here,' Sasha demanded.

He didn't move.

'Cal, come on!'

'We have to help.'

'We can't stay here. This wasn't a coincidence. Think!'

'I don't understand.'

'That bomb was meant for us.'

'Don't be stupid,' he said. 'Your father wouldn't drop a bomb on *you*.'

57

'Assuming he knew I was with you. Besides, the Drones are all programmed; he doesn't oversee everything. If he gave the command to the Watchhouse, that'd be enough. The moment your chip died you became his enemy, Cal. And now you've seen the truth he won't rest until he knows you are dead.'

Cal didn't want to believe her, wanted to argue that Trent had no way of knowing he'd even seen the truth, not now his Neurochip was gone, he wasn't connected to the *Neuralnet*, but she was right on one point, the moment his chip went dead he'd become Marshall Trent's enemy. He'd broken his promise. He'd thrown away his second chance. If the bomb had been meant for him, then it was his house at the centre of the blast, and it would be no more than a pile of burning rubble. Was someone right now trying to pull his father from the wreckage? And even if it wasn't his house, even if his father was fine, he'd be trying to find Cal. Cal wished he'd never clambered out of that window. How could he have left him like that? He had to go home. There was no way he could just ignore what had happened, not if it was his fault.

'I've got to go back.'

'Are you kidding me?'

'My dad's back there.'

'I'm sorry, Cal. Really, I am. But we've got to get as far away from here as we can. I know he's your dad, but the *worst* thing we can do is go back to your place. Drones will be watching it. The area will be crawling with Enforcers in case you somehow emerge from the ruins. Going back would be suicide.'

'I can't just leave him.'

'That's exactly what you have to do if you want to keep him safe. If he's caught with us, then he'll be arrested, too. You heard what my father said, he'll be an enemy of the state. As long as we keep away from him he's got a chance.'

'But what if it was my house?'

'Then you can't help him,' she said.

That was true of course, but it didn't make running any easier.

He was still clutching the rucksack, the laptop inside. There was more on it he hadn't seen. He had to keep it safe. It was the only way he'd understand exactly what he'd been sucked into, and, maybe more importantly, why.

'Come on,' Sasha urged.

It was easier to leave than it was to stay behind once they were caught up in the tide of bodies funnelling along the narrow streets. Mothers clutched their children close to them, trying to get them to safety. He saw a father holding a crying toddler in his arms. It was desperate, frightening. The world they all believed in had shattered. This wasn't a film set with its scenery caving in. As Cal and Sasha moved further and further away, though, they risked a few backwards glances to see how large the crowd of evacuees had grown.

Suddenly a huge infoscreen ahead of them burst into life and people slowed then stopped, conditioned to listen when Marshall Trent spoke. Others came up behind them, barging into their backs. Parents hushed their children. Everyone wanted to hear what Marshall Trent had to say. They wanted to know how he was going to keep them safe.

'Citizens!' Trent's voice boomed even before his image had formed on the screen. 'As many of you have already heard, tonight there has been a cowardly Anarchist attack in one of the Communities. Emergency services along with volunteers are working hard to help survivors.'

The image changed to show men and women in hard hats and protective clothing working alongside ordinary people as they battled to clear the rubble.

The picture only remained on the screen for a moment.

That's not true, Cal thought. Marshall Trent was lying to them. He hadn't heard a single siren. There hadn't been time for any emergency vehicles to come to their aid yet. Marshall Trent was telling people what they wanted to hear.

'Anarchists,' he heard someone close by say.

The word rang inside his head like a warning bell.

Sasha pulled at him, forcing her way through the massed ranks of people completely enthralled with what was being shown on the big screens. This wasn't something happening halfway round the world or even in a city in their own country that was too far away to visit. The terror was on their own doorstep.

Cal followed in Sasha's wake, hearing muttered complaints, but in the main everyone just stared at the screen captivated by Marshall Trent.

It didn't look like a fake broadcast this time. The images showed the streets around them.

Cal scanned the upturned faces, hoping to catch a glimpse of his father, then he realised if the broadcast was genuine his best chance of seeing him was up on the big screen. Why was Trent saying that it was a terrorist attack?

An instant later Cal had his answer. His own face appeared on the screen.

The picture had been taken earlier in the day, when he'd thrown his backpack between Sasha and the Enforcer's baton. It must have been, but that wasn't what it showed. It had been doctored.

He stopped in his tracks despite Sasha's best efforts to keep him moving. 'What?' he said, not even realising the word had left his lips. No one was paying any attention to him, though. Up on the screen they watched an Anarchist run from an explosion, glancing over his shoulder at his handywork. There it was held, a moment frozen in time, his face staring back at him. Cal's heart skipped a beat and he felt his knees start to buckle.

'Do not be fooled by appearances,' Trent's voice boomed. 'This youth is our enemy. And he is an enemy of the worst sort, one raised in the heart of a good family, given all the chances only one of our own could have. And this is how he repays our kindness. His name is Callaghan Jones and he is responsible for the death and destruction wrought in the heart of one of our Communities. He must pay for his crimes.'

No one was looking at him. Yet.

He needed to get out of there but he couldn't move.

Another change of image on the screen. He saw two rescue workers lifting someone from the wreckage. For an instant the camera showed the wounds to a young woman's face and chest. There was no way she could have survived the injuries. Cal felt, as much as heard, the collective gasps of the people around him.

'We need to go,' Sasha whispered urgently in his ear.

She was right. Once the crowd realised he was the so-called Anarchist they'd be out for his blood. These were people he'd known all his life – friends, neighbours – but as far as they were concerned Marshall Trent had just confirmed that he was the very worst kind of terrorist, a familiar enemy.

The screen changed again, this time back to a close-up of him, his name in large letters beneath. There was no mistaking it was him, either. Cal almost believed it himself. He ducked his head down and tried to ease his way out of the press of bodies without drawing attention to himself. He wanted to be invisible.

'Callaghan Jones is considered armed and dangerous. If you see him make a report via the *Neuralnet*. Do not risk approaching him. Let the Enforcers do their jobs. Callaghan Jones must be apprehended as quickly as possible. He cannot be allowed to cause more damage to our Communities. We are together in this, my friends. Hurt one of us, you hurt all of us.

Betray one of us, you betray all of us. And this is a betrayal of the worst kind. It cuts us deep because we believe in second chances. But in Callaghan Jones we made a mistake. We have known for some time who his mother was, but we decided the boy should not be judged by his mother's crimes. We gave him the opportunity to grow up without that burden, without even the knowledge of the blood he shared. We were wrong and now we are paying the price for our kindness.'

He was almost on the fringes of the crowd when his face was replaced by that of a woman. It was an ordinary woman, an ordinary face, but the way the spectators reacted to it could just as easily have been the face of pure evil. 'This was the boy's mother, Anna Jones, a terrorist eliminated by our Enforcers, but only after a series of bombings led to the deaths of ninety-seven Citizens. It is clear that this youth is also beyond redemption.'

A terrorist? His mother? Cal's head spun at the thought.

The gathering hung on Trent's every word. He could feel the mood shifting. They were angry. They blamed him.

Suddenly he was afraid of them. He pulled up the hood of his jacket and kept his head down, not looking at the screen at all now. His only thought was to wriggle through the gaps between the people and find a way out of the mob. He was right on the edge when Trent fell silent. Cal didn't need to look up to know that the screen was giving the crowd another look at his face. Marshall Trent didn't want them forgetting him.

A murmur started to make its way through the people, growing as it got nearer. They knew exactly who he was and where he lived.

Cal dared to look up, trying to see a way through the press of bodies.

It was a mistake.

'There he is!' someone shouted.

'Grab him!' someone else shouted; someone close.

'Run,' Sasha said, pulling at his arm.

But there was nowhere to run. The mob surged all around them. These people wanted revenge for what they believed he'd done to them. And if that wasn't enough, their Neurochips would be going off like crazy, sending signals out to every Enforcer in the city, telling them where he was.

Chapter 11

Sasha took turn after turn between houses, with no pattern
to her route: left, right, right, right, left, left, just running. She
hurdled discarded rubbish where it spilled out into the street.
Cal slipped on it more than once. The mob followed them,
caught in the ever-narrowing funnel of rat runs as it tried to get
through spaces that were barely wide enough for one man to
squeeze through. At every turn Sasha threw more obstacles into
their path.

Cal risked a glance backwards and almost stumbled as he
did. He gripped the rucksack's strap and ploughed on. The
mob was gaining on them, but not by much. When he turned
back his heart skipped a beat: Sasha was nowhere to be seen.
He panicked. Looking left and right frantically to try to catch a
glimpse of her, or somewhere she could have disappeared into,
down or through. Less than a dozen strides later he crossed
a narrow junction between houses and caught a glimpse of
her climbing the fire escape of one of the SPUs. Cal had never
been inside one of the single-person accommodation units, but
imagined them like cattle stalls for people, with twenty people
living in a building that was smaller than his own home.

'Come on,' she called down to him.

He jumped and grabbed the lowest rung of the ladder that
hung metres above his outstretched fingers. He hauled himself
up, his feet on the first rung when the leader of the mob came
round the corner. Cal scrambled up as quickly as he could, the
rough surface of the rust-pitted metal biting into his hands. He
tried to ignore the pain, but every time he reached for the next
handhold it increased. He couldn't afford to slow down, so Cal
kept looking upwards, concentrating on Sasha. She climbed
effortlessly. He realised again how strong and how fit she was.

The wind swirled around him.

A shower of rust fell on to his face. He turned away just in time to protect his eyes.

The ladder shook and groaned under the extra weight as the front man began to climb up after them. Cal glanced down and saw a familiar face looking up at him. It was one of his neighbours. The father of one of his friends.

'Don't be stupid, Cal,' the man called up to him.

There were about thirty men on the ground below him.

'It's all lies,' Cal told him. He'd known the man for most of his life. He trusted him. Surely he'd believe him. It was the truth, after all. He hadn't done any of the things he was accused of. In the distance he heard the clamour of the mob still baying for his blood. There must have been a hundred more people coming. He wouldn't be able to talk his way out of this. He looked up again. Sasha was now clambering on to the roof.

The ladder juddered again as someone else joined in the chase.

Metal bolts that had never been intended to remain in place for anywhere near as long as they had struggled to hold the weight.

He breathed in concrete dust as a shower spilled down from a bolt threatening to break. It creaked and groaned again, the old metal in danger of pulling away from the wall.

It wasn't going to hold.

It was a long way down. But Cal couldn't go back. He had to go higher.

The wind buffeted him, trying to bully him into letting go of the ladder.

The pins holding the ladder in the wall groaned alarmingly.

Sasha looked down over the rooftop, holding out a hand for him to grasp, but he was too far down to reach it.

He felt a hand snag at his heels. Before it could pull him down he wrenched his ankle free and climbed. Fast. The ladder groaned under the sudden movement. It was only going to hold for a few seconds more before the whole thing gave way and they were left with a couple of seconds to learn how to fly or die.

And then someone else joined them on the ladder. There was no way it would be able to support them all. He had to reach the top.

He grasped the rung above his head and hauled himself up a few more precious metres. Then again, and again, the man beneath him calling out, 'Stop being stupid, Cal. We need to go back to your dad's. Everything's going to be OK. Trust me.'

But it wasn't going to be OK.

It was never going to be OK again.

Sasha's hand grabbed his and she started to haul him up on to the roof. With his belly flat on the rooftop, Cal kicked out at the hand that was trying to pull him back, and one of ladder's bolts shrieked, giving way completely. It came free of the weeping cement, and fell, clattering down towards the ground. It hit one of the men on the way down, catching him on the cheek. His cry was as much in surprise as pain, but he instinctively pulled back, shifting his weight and changing the strain on the metal that was already failing.

Another bolt sheared its housing and the fire escape peeled away from the building.

The first man looked up at Cal as though forgetting why he'd been chasing him and reached out with his right hand. *'Help me, boy, please, I'm begging you . . . For the love of –'*

But Cal never heard what it was for the love of. There was nothing he could do. He had stretched out, but the ladder was already bowing backwards and carrying the man out of reach.

Cal moved away from the edge. There was nothing he could do.

He could still hear the cries for help when Sasha tugged at him again, keeping him moving.

There were three blocks of SPUs in a row, but the third had fallen into such a state of decay and disrepair that it was abandoned. Little more than a rotten husk remained. These SPUs had been the worst of the emergency housing when they'd gone up, but now they were lethal, riddled with chemicals that seeped through the stones, poisoning the air even as they ate away at the structures, undermining their integrity. When they finally fell it would be a mercy, but until then it was where the government hid the poorest of the poor.

'Where now?' he asked, looking at the crumbling concrete in front of them and down at the gaps between buildings. It was a long way down. 'And don't say we jump.'

Sasha moved to the centre of the roof. She turned in a full circle. Cal did the same. There didn't appear to be any way off. They were trapped.

He saw a steel door between some air vents. Roof access. Probably for the satellite receivers and communications dishes. It was locked from the inside. But that didn't mean people wouldn't be climbing the stairs right now, looking to throw them off the roof.

'We jump,' she said.

'I asked you not to say that.'

Before he could stop her, Sasha took off running, head down until the last possible second, and then she launched herself off the edge of the building, kicking forward. And she was still running somehow as though on an invisible bridge. Then she stumbled and fell, sprawling across the cement rooftop on the other side.

'Up there!' someone shouted from below. 'There he is!'

Cal turned to see the roof-access door open and a brute of a man in the doorway, a weapon of some kind, a pipe or chunk of wood, in his hand.

'Cal!' Sasha shouted across the rooftop.

Cal took a step closer to the edge, peering down at the dizzying drop that lay below him. Then he looked across the gap. The distance between the two buildings was less than three metres, and it dropped maybe five more from one to the other, but he would drop an awful lot further than that if he missed his landing.

Sasha stood on the edge, as though she intended to catch him.

'Stay where you are, kid,' the brute said. 'It's over. You're done. Time to face justice. You hurt one of us, you hurt all of us. Look at what you've done to your own kind, kid, your own people. How can you live with yourself?' Two more men had joined him on the roof.

'Don't be stupid, kid. It doesn't have to end like this,' one of them said, holding out a hand for Cal to take. 'On your knees, hands behind your head. Do it. Now.'

Cal shook his head. 'It's all lies . . . I didn't . . . I'm not . . .'

Cal started to walk towards them, measuring out each step carefully as he moved away from the edge. 'I didn't do this,' he said, on the ninth step. Before they could react he turned on his heels and ran for all he was worth. He ran for his life, knowing there was no going back. But even so he almost lost his nerve, his footsteps faltering as he almost overran the edge, but then he threw himself into the air, arms and legs flailing in desperate panic, sure he wasn't going to make it across to the other side.

Then he felt the rooftop under his feet and Sasha pulled him away from the edge. The brute and his companions stood on the far edge of the SPU roof, the gap between them, screaming abuse over at Cal. One had already backed away from the edge and was about to jump after them.

Cal felt every ounce of strength drain from his legs as he turned his back on them.

'Knew you could do it,' she said, grinning.

'Glad someone did,' Cal replied, gasping for breath.

'Now do it again,' she said, and took off running. Without a downwards glance into the chasm between the buildings, she launched herself on to the last roof.

She came down awkwardly. Cal realised there was a hole in the rooftop where fatigue and weathering had broken through, and she'd barely avoided putting her foot through it as she landed. Part of the outer wall had fallen away, too, and leaned against the building he was about to jump off. Wood and insulating fibre lay exposed to the elements. It was only a matter of time before the whole thing came crashing down, and took the other SPUs with it like a line of dominoes. Cal just hoped it wouldn't be in the next few minutes. As he turned and strode back to the centre of the roof, he saw the brute readying to launch himself from the first rooftop.

Cal took a deep breath and started to run.

It was easier second time. He launched himself off the rooftop, his momentum carrying him easily to the other side.

He stumbled as he landed, his feet skidding on the surface that was covered with stones and fragments of cement. The entire structure groaned and creaked as he steadied himself. He didn't know if it was his imagination, but it felt as though the entire building *moved* beneath his feet.

A sharp *crack* filled the air, kick-starting his heart. The roof bowed. The crack sounded again. The sooner they were off the roof the better, but where were they supposed to go? They'd run themselves into a dead end!

He could hear people down below barking orders.

Finally he understood the source of the noise: the rooftop access panel protested violently, but came open. There was nowhere left for them to go. The mob had cornered them. But then he realised Sasha was helping to pull the hatch open. 'Cal!' she shouted, before disappearing inside.

In the distance he heard the whine of an approaching Drone. He couldn't risk being seen up there in the open. He followed her into the ruined building, dreading to learn who or what was waiting for them inside.

'Danni,' he said in surprise as she pulled the hatch closed behind him.

Somehow he'd managed to forget all about her, even though she'd been the one to burn the first chip in his head. Had that only been yesterday? Things were happening so fast and there was nothing he could do to slow them down. It was good to see her. Really good. He grinned despite himself and grabbed her in a fierce bear hug, then let her go and backed off sheepishly while she stared at him, scratching at her blue hair. 'Well, that was unexpected. Good to see you, too.'

She slid a bolt into place, not that it would buy them a lot of time, then urged him down a flight of stairs that would, eventually, bring them out on the ground floor. The building could collapse at any time, and they could hear the mob hammering on the steel doors at the base of the tower block, but he had to trust that she knew what she was doing.

'We have to move *fast*,' Danni said. 'They've dispatched the Drones.'

'I heard one,' Cal said. The two girls paused for a moment, clearly expecting him to say more.

'How far away?' Danni asked.

'No idea. Not far.'

'We've got to get out of here,' Sasha said unnecessarily.

'The Drone won't be able to see us in here,' Cal said, more in the hope than belief that he was right.

'Doesn't need to. Look at this place, a bomb would do everyone a favour. The place is derelict, there's no one here but us, and as far as they are concerned we're Anarchists, and that makes us the enemy.' There was a barely restrained anger in

Sasha's voice as she spoke. Cal knew that when she said 'they', she really meant her father.

With Sasha in the lead, the three of them navigated the dark building. Some light filtered in through cracks in the walls. Danni walked behind him. Cal put his trust in them. They would look after him. They'd get him out of this place.

When they reached the ground floor he saw a damp and rotten door that hung open beneath the stairs. Sasha entered with hesitation. So they weren't going outside at all. They were going underground. Danni offered him a light from a torch she pulled from her pocket. There was a trapdoor, which led to another flight of stairs leading down into the earth.

'Did I mention I'm afraid of the dark?' Cal said, as he looked down into the darkness. He wasn't. He was just trying to lighten the mood. He made stupid jokes when he was frightened.

'Unlucky,' Danni said.

'It could be worse,' Cal said, starting to descend.

'It already is,' Danni said, pulling the rotten door back into place over their heads. 'I wasn't going to tell you, but you should know.'

'Know what?'

'They've got your father.'

Chapter 12

'I can't do this,' Cal said when they finally stopped running.

Danni closed a heavy wooden door behind them.

They walked in single file along a claustrophobic passage. Sasha broke the top off a glow stick and held it above her head for them to follow. They were still descending. The passageway went on for more than a hundred metres, but it seemed endless to Cal. The space was cold and damp. Much colder than above ground. The green-tinged glow stick didn't shed much light on the passageway, but it was enough for him to make out the rough edges of stone and the black patches of hard-packed dirt, which meant the tunnel was manmade. The floor was bare, compacted earth, and every now and then the walls were clad with a variety of materials – everything from chipped tiles to wallpaper – and they came upon doors at irregular intervals, meaning there were more tunnels beneath the Communities. More ways in and more ways out. This was a place for hiding in, not for living in. But when they came upon a chamber with a scattering of furniture and a few rough beds, Cal realised that was exactly how it was used.

It was a huge room, an old dormitory. There were metal shelves along one wall, and five wire-framed beds with no sheets on them and filthy stripped mattresses. He counted four old wooden school chairs around the table in the centre of the room, and four stuffed armchairs that had seen better days grouped together on the other side of it. There was a storm lamp on the table. The glass casing of the lamp was chipped and cracked, so when Danni lit it, it cast curious shadows across the wall.

'Can't do what?' Sasha asked once they had checked that all the doors were locked and secure. It had been more than ten minutes since he'd said anything.

'Stay down here hiding when they've got my dad.'

'Listen to me, Cal. I know my father. He is many things, but he is not a monster. He won't hurt your dad,' Sasha said.

'How can you be so sure?'

'He's my dad. I know him as well as anyone can. He likes power. Hurting people doesn't give you power; the threat of hurting them does. He knows that as long as he's got your dad you'll try to do something. He knows you can't run away now. You won't abandon your father. He's banking on drawing you out into the open. It's you he wants, Cal. He has done ever since he found out who you are.'

'You mean who my mum was?'

Sasha nodded.

'She wasn't a terrorist,' he said, 'I'm not one either. You know that. I can't let my father rot in some prison cell. I can't.'

'But that's exactly what you have to do, Cal. For now, at least. You can't just hand yourself in and hope that he'll let your dad go. That won't help anyone.'

'Then what *should* I do? Tell me.'

It was Danni who answered his question. She'd sunk into one of the battered old armchairs and closed her eyes. 'You should talk to the only person who will know what to do.'

'Who?'

'Buccaneer, of course.'

Cal shook his head. 'How do I even know Buccaneer exists? How do I know it's not another one of Marshall Trent's creations? He needs enemies, he needs someone to blame for everything that goes wrong, so why not just make up a mythical Buccaneer? Blame everything on the Anarchists and people won't blame him for his own failures – like the state of the SPUs. Keep people afraid of some foreign threat and promise them you're the only one who can protect them. That'll keep people in line, won't it?'

'You're learning fast, Cal,' Sasha said. 'Now your eyes are open you're seeing the world as it really is. But Buccaneer is very real. Believe me.'

Cal thought about this for a moment. She was right. His eyes were open. He was questioning things he'd never doubted in the past. It wasn't only because he'd seen the set – which proved that some of the things they had been shown were lies – it was seeing himself portrayed as an Anarchist, seeing the way his friends had turned on him without even trying to find out the truth. It made him nauseous. His entire world had been turned upside-down. Now he didn't know what to believe. The old computer had offered him one possible truth, but was it the whole truth or was it just a lie meant to discredit Marshall Trent? Would Buccaneer be any more truthful than Trent? Or would they tell another kind of lie?

Instead of saying any of this he asked, 'How long are we going to hide here?'

Before either of them could answer the earth rumbled and the foundations of whatever building stood above them shook. Cal knew what the sound meant; a bomb had exploded on the surface. The Drones must have dropped a bomb on the abandoned SPU block they'd used to access the tunnels. Earth crumbled and fell from the compacted soil above them and the cladding on the walls strained and made strange noises, but the room didn't cave in. It withstood the blast. For now.

Cal had visions of the whole thing collapsing on their heads and them suffocating down here. 'Are we safe?'

'Safer than we'd be above ground,' Sasha said, huddling down beside him against one of the fibreboard-clad walls.

'That's not very reassuring.'

'But it's the truth. I won't lie to you, Cal. They'll keep circling with Drones, looking for us, but eventually they'll have to consider the possibility we've given them the slip, and they'll widen the search. That's when we move out.'

'There's enough food and water to keep you going for a few weeks,' Danni added.

'A few weeks?' Cal said, then realised what she had said. 'Hang on, are you planning on leaving me here? Alone?'

The thought terrified him. He imagined being trapped inside this dark damp place on his own, waiting for someone to come for him. Just waiting and waiting and waiting, and going slowly out of his mind. He had no idea where he was. No idea how to escape. He was starting to panic.

Sasha shook her head. 'We won't abandon you, Cal. I promise. We went to a lot of trouble to get you here, away from my father's spies. You've got an important part to play in this war.'

He didn't feel important. He didn't want to feel important. He wanted to feel . . . what? Safe? He wasn't sure he'd ever feel safe again. What would happen the moment he emerged above ground? Would they be waiting for them? It wasn't like the Drones would grow tired or need to sleep. They could replace every one that needed refuelling. They could send Enforcers down to clear the rubble and scan the ruins for signs of life. They couldn't hide forever.

'I still don't get why you think I'm so important,' he said.

In the meagre light he saw Sasha shrug. 'I don't think. I know.'

'But how? How do you know?'

'Because Buccaneer says so.'

'And that's all the proof you need?'

She nodded. 'Buccaneer doesn't lie.'

And that was all she'd say about the subject.

They slept fitfully, Cal tossing and turning and mumbling in his sleep. He woke before the others. He watched Danni sleep, amazed by how small she looked curled up in the chair, and at

Sasha, who talked every now and again, seeming to argue with someone passionately inside her dream. Time passed. Cal had no idea how long. It could have been a couple of hours, it could have been five or six, or even a day. He was hungry. The girls produced a couple of cans of food and while they were able to open them easily enough there was no way of heating the contents so they ate it cold, straight from the tin, using the lid as a spoon.

'I've never tasted anything like this before,' Cal said, scarfing down another mouthful. It was impossible to get a proper view of the contents, which was probably a good thing. He couldn't tell what it was he was eating. Some sort of half-liquid field rations meant to be eaten warm. It was nasty.

'These cans are from before,' Danni said. He didn't want to think about how old that made them. 'We don't think they're produced in this country any more.'

'Where on earth did you find them?'

'This place was some kind of shelter. The buildings replaced ones that had been here before the Last Great Civil War. It took us a long time to clear out the rubble, but now there's a network of tunnels that run most of the way into the city, through a dozen Communities like yours, though some are still blocked. Every time we manage to open up a new section we find another store.'

By the time they'd finished eating, Cal had made up his mind. He wasn't going to sit on his backside waiting. He got to his feet and hefted the rucksack on to his shoulders.

'Where do you think you're going?' Sasha asked.

'Up to you. Take me to meet Buccaneer now or I'll hand myself in. Sitting around like this isn't doing anyone any favours. Who knows how many more lies your father is telling about me while we hide down here in the dark?'

'We have to wait,' said Sasha.

'Who says? You?'

'We should be OK if we're careful,' said Danni, interrupting. 'We'll have to keep a lookout for Drones and hope there aren't any Enforcers out, but for what it's worth I agree with Cal. Besides, who in their right mind would expect Callaghan Jones, public enemy number one, to come walking out?'

Sasha was reluctant to move, but Cal was determined. 'If I've got to leave without you, I will,' he said. It wasn't much of a threat. 'Danni, do you know where to find Buccaneer?'

The girl nodded and without giving Sasha another glance headed towards a door at the far end of the cavernous room.

'Wait for me,' Sasha said scrambling to her feet as the door swung open.

Cal couldn't hold back his smile.

Chapter 13

There was light up ahead. A single point that grew slowly, blindingly to fill the tunnel.

Cal entered the light.

It was so bright it hurt his eyes. He blinked back the sting of tears. Everything around him was blurry and difficult to focus on. It took him a moment to realise Danni had led them out through the power box beneath one of the giant infoscreens.

He tried to get his bearings, looking for landmarks.

They were on the very edge of the Community.

Somehow he'd thought they'd travelled much further than that, but, no, even as he turned in a circle, looking around, he saw the two remaining blocks of SPU housing and a column of smoke rising from the ruined third no more than half a mile away. Somehow the other buildings had withstood the explosion.

Behind the screen the land was overgrown; no one *wanted* to live so close to something that blocked out the sun. Cal looked up at the huge iron pylon, which looked like a giant striding over the rooftops of the city. Most homes had a view of a screen through at least one window. In Cal's it had been his father's bedroom. They had often watched together with the windows open, Marshall Trent's voice coming to them through the dozens of speakers all over the Community. Everyone listened to the broadcasts. They were like salivating dogs answering the ringing of Pavlov's bell come dinner time.

Now Cal found himself fervently hoping that there wouldn't be another broadcast until they were out of the Community. But even then there were screens everywhere. They couldn't hide from them forever.

He could hear the sound of a single Drone in the distance. Had they already given up on finding him alive? Were they just watching with their eyes in the sky for his body to be pulled from the rubble? That would be the money shot, wouldn't it? His body being dragged out, the lens focussing on the bloody wound scabbing behind his ear – up there on the big screen to let the population know they were safe. Marshall Trent had slain the monster that was Callaghan Jones, Anarchist.

He felt sick. 'Where now?' he asked.

The sun was low in the sky. He could see people slowly beginning to return to their homes, either because they sensed the danger was over or to assess the damage. A few hours ago they would have said they had nothing left to lose, but now that was truer than ever. Across the street he saw one of the foodbanks – an empty building that had been claimed by kind souls to collect and distribute food to the hungry and needy. Anyone could find sustenance there. They only opened in the mornings, which meant there wouldn't be a crowd gathering any time soon. That was something at least. That it had come to the stage where the poor couldn't afford to feed themselves and were reliant upon strangers was horrific. That Marshall Trent's news broadcasts sought to blame innocent people for the mess of the Reunited Kingdom was vile. Until today Cal had always believed in Trent, but now all he saw when he looked at the society Marshall Trent had created was fear. A world of fear.

'This way,' said Danni.

Sasha secured the entrance they'd used, working quickly. By the time she was done, it was chained up and looked as though it had never been opened. She said nothing. She was with them, but was obviously reluctant, not liking the unnecessary risks their being out in the open entailed. Cal was certain that if she'd had her way they would still be sitting in the dark waiting for something to happen. Being on the move was better.

'Watch where you step. Walk where I walk, in my footsteps, and no one will be able to tell that we've been this way.' Danni said. She led the way through the undergrowth using stepping stones created from what appeared to be random debris accumulated over the years, but which had obviously been placed to make a path for those who knew it was there. It would have been easier to beat their way through the weeds, but that would have left an obvious trail.

He followed Danni until she stopped. There was an old broken door lying on the ground. She heaved it aside to reveal a metal hatch set into a concrete base. Despite being hidden, it looked well tended, unlike a lot of doors and access hatches that had been left to rot. It opened smoothly when she pulled at it. Cal looked around to make sure that no one had followed them.

'You might want to stand back,' she said, dropping to her knees and spinning the capstan lock – like some kind of ancient safe – until it popped open. She raised the hatch less than a centimetre from the ground, then turned to look at Cal. Cal was sure that he was already standing far enough away, but Sasha, who was behind him, backed up a couple of steps on to a slab of concrete. Cal stood his ground as Danni lifted the metal hatch from its housing.

Rats flew out of the hole like a tidal wave, each trying to be the first to get away. They swarmed over Cal's feet. He tried to jump out of the way, his heart racing as they surged out, but they were everywhere. There wasn't a centimetre of rat-free ground around him, and their slick furry bodies tumbled and scrabbled against his legs as they scrambled over his shoes and each other.

'I tried to tell you,' Danni said as she kicked at the last of the rats making its escape.

'You could have tried a bit harder,' Cal said. He gave a shudder as one rat turned and snapped its jaws at his feet before running away into the undergrowth.

'They're harmless. They're not real. They're *Rattus roboticus*.'

'They're what?'

'Robot Rats,' Sasha said. 'An early warning system Buccaneer built.'

Cal moved forward tentatively to peer down into the space, not believing her. Robot rats? Did she have any idea how utterly mad that sounded? The shaft even stank of vermin. They had to be real. He gagged on the stench when he took a breath. Danni stood beside him, expecting him to descend. But as far as he could tell, the hole was only a few metres deep so there wasn't a lot to descend into.

Another hiding place? Cal wondered.

Sasha abandoned her concrete plinth and crouched beside him, reaching down into the filth and feeling around, moving mulched leaves until she grasped hold of an iron ring. 'You want to give me a hand? You're the one who wanted this, remember.'

'Is it too late to change my mind?' Cal said, earning himself a cuff around the back of the head from a grinning Danni.

'Stop being a big baby,' she said.

Ignoring her, Cal reached into the hole to take hold of the cold metal ring. He pulled hard, heaving it up to reveal a metal ladder set into the lining of the shaft. There was a faint glow below them.

They closed everything behind them, plunging the shaft into absolute darkness. The only relief came from the glow that seemed a long way below them as they climbed slowly down. Danni led the way, Sasha at the rear, with Cal in the middle, protected. With every few metres they descended, more and more lights came into view, which had been virtually invisible from above. Long before they reached the bottom, the accumulation of these small firefly-like lights was enough to illuminate the entire shaft.

Cal tried to look down, but couldn't see much beyond Danni, and the bottom seemed no closer than when they'd started their descent. 'How much further?' he asked, his voice echoing loudly in the cramped confines.

'Almost there,' Danni promised him, the sound of her boots landing on a solid surface and emphasising her words.

Cal looked down to see that she'd stepped away from the ladder. The glow still lay some distance below him and she appeared to be levitating.

It took him a moment to realise that she was standing on some sort of transparent surface.

'Glass?' he asked, steadying himself as he stepped down on to it.

Sasha shook her head. 'Toughened industrial plastic. It's been here for years and hasn't broken yet, if that's what you're worrying about? Jump.'

As though to prove the point Sasha jumped from the ladder when she was still a few rungs short of the transparent platform. It didn't give a millimetre, but even so Cal instinctively grasped the ladder.

'The rats will be back soon, so maybe we should get a move on?' Danni called up to them. 'It can get quite unpleasant down here with them crowding all around you, even if they aren't real.'

He had a sudden image of trying to get back out the way they'd come on, but with the rats streaming down the shaft at the same time. 'Please tell me there's another way out of here,' he said.

'I could,' Danni said, grinning. 'But I'd be lying.'

He dropped down on to the plastic surface and followed the girls into a pipeline that fed off the main shaft.

Swags of electrical cables were looped along the cramped passageway. Fluorescent arrows pointed the way along the walls. He saw the familiar spray-painted circle on the square of the Anarchists painted on a door in front of them. He followed the girls to it.

Danni took her home-made rig from one of her deep pockets and ran some sort of codebreaker on the door. Cal heard a series of notes, then a click as the lock released. She pushed the door open and the shaft filled with light.

This was it. The heart of the uprising. There were answers behind the door. They wouldn't be alone any more, because up until that moment it had felt like him, Sasha and Danni against the world. Three kids. What difference could three kids make?

He stood on the threshold.

This wasn't the rough and ready hiding place of the abandoned cavern beneath the Community with its rusty beds and worn-out mattresses, this place was humming with machinery. The air was *fresh*. The place was clean. There were banks of machines, row after row of powerful but antiquated super computers. There were screens set in the machines, and bigger flat screens on the walls and, in the centre of it all, a rig that was unlike anything Cal had ever seen before. It looked like an aeroplane cockpit with a single pilot's seat in the heart of a rainbow of dangling cables, with a single headset set on a tripod. This was Buccaneer's rig, and it jacked right into the very core of the *Neuralnet*.

The Anarchists' headquarters was something between a fortress, a subterranean palace and a home. They stepped in and the door closed behind them, sealing them inside.

They were expected.

The girls made way for him to walk between them.

'Hello, Cal,' said the woman standing in the middle of the room.

She was crying.

Cal backed up a step, shaking his head.

She had changed a lot in the years since he had last seen her, but there was no way in this life or any other that he'd not recognise her. It didn't matter that every picture he had of her was out of date, trapped in the moment of time when she'd died.

Chapter 14

'I'm sorry, Cal. If it could have been any other way . . . I'd never have gone, but it was the only way I could keep you safe. The world had to believe that I was dead.'

'So you could become Buccaneer?'

'It was more than that.'

'Was it?'

'How long have you been here? Why didn't you ever let me know you were alive? Why didn't you reach out to me? Why did they know you were alive and I didn't?' He was almost yelling as he wheeled round to stab a finger at Sasha and Danni.

'Which question do you want me to answer first?'

'Does Dad know?'

She shook her head. 'I couldn't take the chance. You need to understand, your dad, he's a principled man. He didn't agree with what I was doing. He believed in Marshall Trent's peace. He would have handed me over to Trent and his people if he knew I was alive.'

'You don't mean that!'

'Has he *ever* spoken about me since I left? Even once?'

Now that she mentioned it, he couldn't remember a time when his father had ever spoken about his mother. Cal had asked questions, of course, trying to keep her alive in his mind, but his father had always pushed them aside, changing the subject or promising they'd talk about her when he was older. But they never had, and Cal had stopped asking.

'Were you really a terrorist?' he said.

A smile came to her face, then an easy smile that brought back so many memories. 'Are you?'

He shook his head.

'One man's terrorist is another man's freedom fighter,' she argued.

He understood what she meant. But it was just semantics, wasn't it? She wasn't denying the bombs Marshall Trent had accused her of, or the ninety-seven deaths. So what Trent had said was true, at least in part. Did Trent know she was Buccaneer? Or did he truly believe she was dead? Cal realised he couldn't think of her as his mother. The woman in front of him was Buccaneer.

'How could you leave me?' he asked, knowing he sounded like a child.

'I watched over you, Cal. Every day. All these years. I watched and waited, hoping you'd come and find me, hoping there'd be a time when we'd be reunited, but I couldn't put you in danger. No matter how desperately I wanted to talk to you. Sometimes I could have reached out and touched you, we were so close, but I couldn't do it. I couldn't make your life worse than it already was.'

'But you did manage to put me in danger didn't you? And Dad.'

'Not me, Cal. You chose to help Sasha. I didn't make you do it.'

'How do I know that? How do I know you didn't engineer the whole thing, picking the Watchhouse as a target because you knew it was on my route home, picking the time you knew I'd be standing in the square watching the news stream? I'm there every day. You said you've been watching me. You know that I'm there every day.'

'All that is true, son, but the most important thing is that you chose to help her. That's down to you. Maybe you've got a little bit of your mother in you, after all?'

'I don't even know what I'm supposed to call you. Mum? Buccaneer? I can't call you Anna Jones, because she's dead . . .'

'You can call me whatever you want, Cal. I'm still your mum.'

Cal knew that he should have been delighted his mother was still alive, but right now instead of joy he felt angry. Angry that she hadn't trusted him. Angry that he'd been lied to for most of his life. Angry that she'd chosen this life over him. Angry that she hadn't wanted to be his mother enough to take him with her. He wouldn't have told anyone that she was still alive. He hated that she'd been so close to him all this time without him knowing she was there.

'I'm sorry,' she said, reaching out to lay a hand on his shoulder.

'Don't touch me.'

He backed up a step, shaking his head. Angry. That's what he felt. Angry. Cheated out of a life.

'There are things you don't understand, Cal. Things you don't know about.'

'Like the stuff on the laptop you sent me?' He held her gaze, determined not to be the first one to blink. He'd wait as long as it took, but she was going to tell him everything before he left this room. She owed him that much.

'We should leave them to it,' Danni said to Sasha. 'Give them some quality mother–son time.'

Danni flashed him a smile as they left.

His breath caught in his throat as he tried to smile back. It was hard.

He was glad that they were going. There were questions he wanted to ask that his mother wouldn't answer with an audience.

'You're right,' his mum said when they were alone. 'This is all my fault. I don't just mean what's happened to you and your dad.'

'Sasha and Danni?'

'Everyone.'

'What do you mean?'

'Exactly what I said. Everyone.'

Cal waited, not understanding what she was saying.

He could see the sadness in her eyes. He needed to ask the right questions, but had no idea what they were. 'Tell me,' he said instead, hoping that would be enough.

'You know the chip you had in your head?'

'Which one?'

'Either of them. Both of them. They're my fault. You wouldn't have had them if it hadn't been for me.'

He shook his head. 'Everyone's got one. They don't have anything to do with you.'

'I invented them, Cal,' she said. 'I didn't understand how Marshall Trent would use them until it was too late, but it's my fault. I'm the one who put them in everyone's heads.'

He shook his head again. 'No. That's impossible. People have had these things since the Last Great Civil War. You couldn't have invented them.'

'I changed them. Improved them. I made them do more than just give you a connection to the *Neuralnet*. I made them two-way. I showed Trent how you could use them to collect and store memories.'

'What's the point of that?' Cal asked.

'My idea was to preserve knowledge. As people get older they start to forget. There are diseases like Alzheimer's that rob people of who they were, so they can't even remember who they are, how they fit into the world . . . it was a way of keeping them alive. But Trent twisted my research. He wanted to retrieve people's memories and use them to locate anyone who was plotting against his new government. But that's not how it was meant to be used.'

'Why not?' Cal asked.

'It's invasive. Manipulative. It assumes everyone is plotting. It's paranoid. We deserve better. We deserve to be trusted,' she said.

But to Cal the idea that everyone was being watched was something he'd always accepted. It was just part of life. It didn't matter if it was his mother who'd invented the chip that allowed it to happen. 'The only people who object to being watched are the ones who have something to hide,' he said, and then made the logical leap to why Buccaneer burned the chips out of her acolytes. 'That's why you get rid of their chips, isn't it? Because you don't want them to be seen doing something wrong.'

'It's more than that,' she said. 'You need to understand that Marshall Trent is using the chips for so much more than monitoring people. He can use them to influence people without them even knowing it's happening. That's how he's stayed in power for so long. No one can stand up to him, not while they have those chips in their heads. If it hadn't been for me, the world wouldn't be in the state it's in. People wouldn't be hanging on to the word of Trent like he's some kind of all-knowing, all-powerful being. I want to put this right. I want to stop it all. I have to. Or die trying.'

'But how can you? The Neurochip is in everybody's heads. Everybody. That's millions of people, all joined together. Everything they think being streamed back to Marshall Trent. Every thought of rebellion betraying them before they have a chance to act upon it. It's impossible. Dad's in one of Trent's prisons because of you. You talk about putting this right, well, Dad needs your help, so help him. Get him out of there.'

'I can't,' she admitted, sadness in her voice. In those two words Cal knew just how much she still cared, and it broke his heart. 'But I think that you can.'

Chapter 15

Cal half-expected a welcoming committee when he reached the plaza in the centre of New Edgehill.

So much had happened since he'd last stood in the same spot, yet it had only been a couple of days ago. He looked up at the iron pylon supporting the huge infoscreen, which covered the width of the Watchhouse's lowest floors. There was no news stream offering lies about him this morning, but he wasn't naive, they would come. The tower itself clawed up at the sky, seeming bonier than ever to Cal. He lurked in the shadows, steeling himself. It was a short walk around the plaza in terms of distance. It was a long walk in terms of the kind of emotional strength it demanded. The morning sun glinted off the glass doors, making them look like particularly sharp teeth in a wicked grin.

Cal had slept badly in the bed that Buccaneer had provided, but he was rested.

He knew what he had to do. His stomach growled as he looked up at the building. He hadn't eaten since the tin of whatever it was he'd scarfed down in the tunnels the day before. There'd been plenty of food in Buccaneer's bunker but he hadn't been able to face eating. He was frightened.

The plaza was almost empty. A handful of people made their way across the ornate floor, their feet scuffing the surface that had cost more than most Citizens earned in a year, maybe even a lifetime. The pink and white marble shone in the early-morning sunshine, carrying a sheen like water on its surface. More Citizens were following the walkways that skirted the plaza, as though reluctant to stand on the precious surface.

Cal took a deep breath and stepped out of the shadows. There was no turning back now.

He was sure someone would recognise him and call out his name, but no one challenged him. They were all too busy rushing about, heads down, either lost in their own thoughts or catching up with the goings on of the world through their rigs or accessing the *Neuralnet* to waste time on their commute – no time for the real world around them. Some perverse part of Cal wanted to raise his arms and shout out that he wasn't afraid of Marshall Trent, but Buccaneer had told him exactly what he must do to set his father free and drilled into him that he mustn't deviate from the plan.

Cal knew that he would be less conspicuous if he made his way round the plaza, tucking himself close to the buildings on its edge. But less conspicuous didn't mean a smaller chance of being recognised. He needed to do this on his own terms, not at the will of some angry mob if the cries went up that an Anarchist was there, or by being brought in by Enforcers as though still on the run. He was turning himself in to set his father free. He had to be seen to surrender.

He kept his head low with his hood pulled up.

The infoscreen hummed into life. The thirty or so people in the plaza stopped, enthralled by the image of Trent's face as it materialised. Everyone apart from Cal.

Cal had never noticed it before, but now he was beginning to understand. It wasn't that they were interested. It was as though they were responding to a programmed command: the broadcast came on and, no matter how trivial the content, they stopped. Marshall Trent had absolute control over them. Cal glanced around. No one was looking at him. He knew they wouldn't be. They were all staring at the screen. How could he have been so blind all this time? How could he not have seen what was happening all around him?

Open Your Eyes. He recalled that first message and realised just how important it was on so many levels. His eyes were open now and he didn't like what he was seeing.

'Citizens –' the familiar voice of Marshall Trent boomed out across the plaza – 'yesterday brought the tragic news of another atrocity committed by Anarchists against one of our own Communities here in New Edgehill, the heart of the Isles. The mastermind behind the attack was none other than the Anarchist known as Buccaneer. Irrefutable evidence has come into my hands that the boy, Callaghan Jones, is Buccaneer's puppet.'

Cal saw his face fill the screen again. He cast another furtive look around, but no one appeared to have seen him. People peered at the screen, none of them taking their eyes from it. He needed to move now. To get across the square to the Watchhouse while Marshall Trent's words commanded their absolute attention. He slipped between onlookers, careful not to touch or push them as he wriggled through gaps that were too narrow. As he drew closer to the screen the gaps became smaller as people crowded together.

Cal couldn't help himself. He looked up at the screen and saw himself looking down on the plaza. He stood in line with the front row. It was impossible not to believe the lies Trent was telling about him. He bit down on his lower lip as the image of his mother lying dead on the ground appeared. He now knew she wasn't dead, no matter what Trent said. He still didn't know how he felt about the fact she'd lied to him all these years. It would be a long time until he came to terms with it, he thought, looking at her up on the screen, but they had that time now, didn't they?

'The boy is acting under the belief that he is seeking revenge against society for the death of his mother. He does not know the truth. He needs to be brought into custody so we can help him understand. There is still a chance to save this boy, but only if we as a society choose to save him. The question is, my friends, does he deserve to be saved?'

The image changed again to show a line of body bags on the ground where the debris from an explosion had been cleared away. He recognised some of the buildings in the background. This was the SPU that had been taken out by Trent's Drones last night.

'Twenty-seven dead . . . Killed by a misguided child . . .'

He wasn't a child.

He wasn't responsible.

And for all he knew there weren't even bodies inside those bags.

'Do we spare him?'

All around the plaza the gathered people cried out as one, 'No!'

Thirty voices echoed all across the city by thousands upon thousands more all crying out that same word.

Marshall Trent had his answer. It was the will of the people.

Cal stepped forward again, out of the line, isolating himself just as the transmission came to an end. He took a step forward, and another, and another until he reached the steps that led up from the marble ground to the glass doors of the Watchhouse, which served as Marshall Trent's headquarters here in the city. No turning back now.

Halfway up the steps Cal fell to his knees.

Buccaneer had told him to expect Drones circling the area, the eyes and ears of the Enforcers, but there was no sign of the fake birds up in the sky. In the momentary silence after the hum of the screen fell away there was only the sound of footsteps moving away as people began to return to what they had been doing. No one even noticed Cal kneeling on the steps, waiting.

He placed his hands on his head and waited.

Slowly the doors swung open.

Chapter 16

Sasha watched as the boy walked slowly up the steps to the Watchhouse's glass doors.

She was a hundred metres away across the plaza, close enough to see everything, far enough away to run if she needed to.

Buccaneer hadn't wanted her to go, but she needed to see him.

She couldn't understand why the leader of the Anarchists was putting so much faith in him when they had only just met, but she was. She'd told Sasha that anarchy flowed in his veins. That he was born to do this. It was different for him. Buccaneer trusted Cal more than she trusted her. She realised what she was feeling: jealousy.

They'd left Buccaneer and Cal together for a couple of hours while Danni had shown her how to operate a remote broadcasting unit, a vital part of what had to happen next, if they were going to succeed. In those two hours the mother and son had become thicker than thieves. How else could she have convinced him to go in there and face being purged?

Anarchy flowed in his blood? It didn't matter what Buccaneer asked her to do, Sasha was always going to feel like an outsider. She would never be completely trusted because of her father.

She'd brought Cal in because Buccaneer had asked her to. Maybe it was a test. If it was she should have passed with flying colours. But nothing had changed. She was still being kept at arm's length.

Her heart raced as the doors opened and the Enforcers stepped out into the open. She could hear the servos of their armour hissing as they marched down the stairs to circle him. Five, flanked by five more, then five more until she lost sight of Cal there on his knees, hands behind his head. The world seemed to stop around her. Half the people in the plaza stopped to watch, while others deliberately turned away, not wanting to see. That was the nature of her father's rule: hear no evil, see no evil, speak no evil and pretend no evil exists even when it is right there in front of you dressed up in the body armour of an Enforcer.

Sasha felt a moment of panic when her father appeared in the doorway by Cal.

She pressed herself deeper into the shadows of the grocer's shop doorway, trying to make herself invisible. It was one of the few friendly places in the city, and simply by being there in the doorway she was jeopardising their ally's safety. She shouldn't be there.

Marshall Trent saw her across the plaza, but did nothing. He didn't see her as a threat. Even he paid more attention to Cal. She wanted to scream, 'Open your eyes! Look at me!' but she didn't. It was too important for that. Cal needed to get inside. Everything depended upon that happening.

'Time to go,' Danni said at her shoulder.

Sasha hadn't even realised that the blue-haired hacker had followed her. Maybe she hadn't, maybe she had known where she was going? Or maybe Buccaneer had told Danni where to find her?

The shopkeeper nodded to the pair of them as they walked inside.

He was a friend. One of Marshall Trent's familiar enemies. A good man. 'Quickly,' he said. 'Out of sight. You're not safe here, not with so many Enforcers out there.'

Neither of the girls argued. They moved through the stacks of food to the stairs at the back of the store, out of sight of the window.

'I still don't understand why it's so important that Cal hands himself in. Why now?' Sasha asked.

Danni shrugged and turned away. 'I don't ask questions. I just do what I'm told. Buccaneer's expecting you. Everything hinges on you. The timing is crucial. She's trusting you.' There was something about the way she said that last line, *She's trusting you,* that sounded almost accusatory, like how could she possibly trust Marshall Trent's daughter?

Even now – more than ever – she still had to prove herself.

Chapter 17

Enforcers swarmed out of the Watchhouse – two, four, ten, twelve, twenty, and they kept coming, until there was what felt to Cal like a small army of android warriors standing in the plaza. More than Cal even knew existed spilled out and circled him. They left him no means of escape – not that he planned to.

The only place in the world he wanted to be was inside that building.

The Enforcers slowed, the hiss and stamp of their regimented march falling silent. A pathway opened up between their ranks leading up to the door. For a moment, the only sound was the steady fall of many human footsteps moving towards the door.

Behind him the gathered crowd took up the chant, 'Kill him! Kill the Anarchist!' and it was absolutely terrifying.

Cal looked up to see a lone figure standing in the doorway.

There was no mistaking even the silhouette of Marshall Trent.

'Well, well, well, the little Anarchist returns,' Trent said. 'Can you hear them calling for your blood, Callaghan? They don't think I should spare you. What do you think I should do?'

Cal didn't say anything.

'I shall enjoy reprogramming you,' Trent said. And to the Enforcers he added, 'Bring him in.'

Cal tried to keep his feet off the ground as they lifted him, but his toes caught on each step as he was dragged towards the doorway.

At the top of the steps he made eye contact with Marshall Trent. Maybe it was stupid, but he wanted the dictator to know that he was here of his own free will. Trent nodded, perhaps an acknowledgement, and stepped aside to let the Enforcers haul him inside.

Buccaneer had promised him there was nothing to be afraid of here, but it was an empty promise. How could she possibly know what would happen to him? But then, she'd known Trent would want to reprogram him, hadn't she?

Even if everything went according to plan and Marshall Trent let his father go, he knew that there was no guarantee he would leave this place alive. It was a risk he was willing to take.

They were barely inside the building when the doors hissed closed behind them. Cal heard magnetic bolts firing into place, locking the Watchhouse down. He felt something cold press against his neck. There was a moment of pain followed by sudden blackness that seemed to last forever.

He heard a voice calling out to him in the darkness. A word. A name? Callaghan. Cal. Callaghan. Was it his name or was it just sounds? He couldn't focus on it. His head ached. The inside of his skull throbbed behind his eyes. Over and over – Cal, Callaghan, Callaghan, Cal – until it stopped making any sense.

He tried to open his eyes, but the blindingly bright light only intensified the pain.

He was in a white room. He didn't want the white. He wanted black. He wanted darkness.

He welcomed the darkness.

He wanted to hide inside it.

But the voice grew more and more insistent.

He opened his eyes to see a face looking down at him. There was a white mask over his mouth. All he could see, really see, were the eyes looking down at him. Was that pity in them? Cal closed his eyes again, trying to remember who he was, where he was, why he was there. It was important he remembered. But nothing made any sense. His head felt empty. No matter how hard he tried he couldn't remember a thing.

He wasn't there.

He wasn't inside his own head.

He had no idea who he was.

He couldn't remember the last thing he'd eaten, the colour of his own eyes, the size of his feet or where he lived. He couldn't remember his parents' faces. He couldn't remember the first girl he'd kissed or if he'd even kissed a girl. Nothing. Callaghan Jones wasn't inside his own head. He didn't live there anymore. And that was terrifying.

A tear formed in his eye and slid down the side of his face.

Even that was a new experience . . . the first time he could remember ever crying.

But that one sensation seemed to spark a memory. He had no idea what it meant, but he clung on to it desperately: a sequence of numbers. They rattled around inside his head, fixed in a sequence, always the same sequence, so it had to have meaning even if he didn't know what that was. It *had* to be important. Why else had it survived the purge? This was more important than his own name.

The throbbing began to die down. He tried to open his eyes again. The face still glared down at him, too close to his own. He attempted to turn his head away, but felt something tugging at a patch of skin behind his ear.

'Do you know who I am?'

'No,' Cal said. The word felt strange on his tongue.

Something beeped – just once – and the man made a note on a console he held in front of him.

'Do you know who *you* are?' The pity in his eyes was even more pronounced as he asked this.

Cal tried again, but couldn't find a name that fit. He tried the one word he'd heard since waking. 'Cal,' he said. Another beep, another note on the pad.

'Do you know what the date is, Cal?'

'Date?'

'Yes. Do you know what the date is?'

'No.' Another beep. He was learning something new. The beeps confirmed he was telling the truth. One for the truth. Silence for a lie? Was the sequence of numbers in his head a date? Why would the only thing he could remember be a date? No. It couldn't be. The number was a secret, never to be told.

'Do you know where you are?'

'No.' He pulled against the restraints, but he couldn't move his head at all. Pain blossomed inside his skull, sending a wave of nausea through him. There was no end to it. He couldn't remember a time without pain. 'I don't know anything. Why do you keep asking me questions?'

'To be sure,' the man answered.

'Of what?'

'To be sure that the procedure was a success.'

'I don't understand . . .' He felt the pain again.

The more agitated he became the more intense the throbbing became, until it felt like a bomb was going off inside his brain.

'Relax, Cal, it's not important.'

It made no sense.

Nothing did.

The man was talking in riddles.

'What have you done to me?'

'You were a troubled soul, Cal. But now you have been saved.'

Saved?

From what?

He tried to think, but the only thing going through his mind was the sequence of numbers. They danced across his mind in a never-ending stream of numerals, rising and falling in time with the agony inside his head.

Chapter 18

When he woke again he had been moved. He wasn't in the white room.

Instead of lying down he was almost upright. He couldn't move his arms or legs. He saw tubes and wires attached to different parts of his body, keeping it alive with a constant supply of nutrition in liquid form, regulating his breathing and other bodily functions so he need never leave this coffin.

He tried to move his head but the restraints prevented him from looking down.

His prison was made from a clear plastic casing. There was someone outside the pod moving around, watching him, and beyond them other cases like his.

Was this some kind of hospital?

What was the matter with him?

Was he sick?

Contagious?

Dying?

Or was it a prison?

What was his crime?

What had he done to be put here?

Was that what the man had meant when he had said he'd been saved?

Was he some kind of criminal?

A menace to society?

He couldn't remember.

He couldn't remember anything except that sequence of numbers.

He wanted to scream.

As he became more and more aware, he realised how much he didn't know, how little was in his memory. Whenever he tried to concentrate on anything, the only thing that existed was a line of numbers, as if they were indelibly printed on his brainstem.

The man had talked about a procedure. Had they wiped his memory, like they were reformatting his hard drive? Cleaning him out for a reboot? Was that even possible?

Did he have a virus? Were they saving him? Was that what this was all about? He was being saved?

Then why had the numbers survived the purge? Were they the source of the virus? Were they what was wrong with him?

A sudden pain jolted Cal from his daydreaming. His mind swarmed with images. Faces in crowds, photographs, close-ups of men and women together and apart; but none of them meant anything to him. He tried to concentrate on them, willing himself to remember if he'd ever known these people, and slowly he began to see similarities. There were faces that appeared in more than one picture. Then he started to notice them in groups, and as the groups became crowds he was still able to pick them out. Cal had no idea what this meant, if it meant anything, or how the pictures were even appearing inside his head. They just kept flashing through his mind faster and faster until it physically hurt to try to focus on them.

'Stop it!' he begged. 'Please. Stop. Please.' He couldn't be sure if the words came from his mouth or existed only inside his head. He wasn't even sure there was a difference any more.

Cal opened his eyes. He could see shapes moving beyond the pictures. Someone was coming towards him. It took a second or two for the shape to resolve into the man in the white coat. He tapped on the panel in front of Cal's face, shrugged then walked away.

'Let me out!' Cal tried to shout, but even though he heard the words he could see in his reflection that his lips weren't moving.

He tried to move his arms, to bang on the glass, but he had no control over his limbs. He couldn't so much as twitch a finger. Nothing would respond.

Had his eyelids been closed? Or had his brain swum into focus and made it feel like he'd opened his eyes?

At last the pictures stopped flashing across his mind, but in their place was the string of numbers. That same sequence streamed through his mind over and over, until he could hear as well as see them. He wanted to clamp his hands over his ears and silence them before his head exploded, but he still couldn't move. Part of Cal knew he *needed* to know what those numbers meant. Until he did, they were just a reminder that he knew nothing.

A man's face appeared in his head.

There was something familiar about it.

This wasn't a stranger.

But . . . if not a stranger . . . then who?

He must have seen him before . . .

Somewhere.

Where?

Was it someone he should know?

Why couldn't he even guess?

He couldn't stop himself. His mind began to riffle through the pictures he had already seen, bringing them back up into his field of vision one after another, faster and faster as he flicked through them, searching for one with the same face. There was more than one. He isolated them, setting them aside into a quarantined segment of his mind, unsure how he was able to do it. Cal had no idea who the man was; there was nothing in any of the pictures that hinted at his identity, although there was plenty he could use to learn about the man, he realised. The places he was pictured, the clothing he wore, the fact that in most he had stubble rather than a clean shave – these were little fragments that could be used to build a jigsaw. Cal tried to concentrate on these tiny details, building a picture of his own from the components at his disposal, but his failure only served to make him feel more frustrated.

His head had been almost empty when he'd awoken; these pictures, these memories had been implanted in the short time he'd been conscious. They weren't his. And as that thought crossed his mind, the faces disappeared, as though punishing him for questioning them.

Cal tried to remember what the face inside his mind had looked like, but it was impossible. The image was gone. Cal's head was empty again. He'd blinked and lost him and now he was gone forever. There was nothing left in his head . . . and yet . . . and yet . . . he knew that it had been a picture of a man, so it hadn't gone completely. Even though he couldn't bring it back into focus, he knew what it had been so he hadn't forgotten.

He tried a different approach, coming at the memory sideways. There had been another picture of the same man with a woman. He focussed on her instead. She was smiling. He assumed she was happy, but that was all he could remember. She was just a faint shadow where there had been two faces in his mind. No matter how hard he tried to recreate it, her face and the man's beside her were always out of reach. It was somewhere in that vast gallery he'd sifted through, but how was he supposed to find someone when he had no idea what he looked like?

Another photo, another search, a woman this time. He tried to lock her features in his memory, concentrating on the space between her eyes, the shape of her nose, the curve of her smile, the colour of her lipstick, the blush of her cheeks. He knew the picture would disappear once he found her in the gallery of other images. It was vital he cling on to every tiny detail, even the most insignificant, while his mind carried on whirring and sifting through the endless store of images on file.

Focus. Concentrate. Don't lose her. Don't let her go.

He repeated this over and over, trying to tie the words in with the image somehow so that one might bring the other back. It wasn't exactly sophisticated, but if it worked he'd be able to remember her face as if he'd made a copy of it. Sound and vision. She had to be important. Why else was he seeing her? That *made* her important. *Which came first, the chicken or the egg?* Cal thought, not remembering where he'd heard that.

Cal processed the image again, repeating the search. This time, as his mind raced through the pictures, things within them were tagged with number sequences identifying them. Some were simple, associating the species of bird in the sky in the background, or trees and street locations, while others were longer and tagged people with their PIDs.

It was as though he was learning new capabilities all the time. With these numbers what else could he learn about these people? Everything. If he knew where to look. For now he concentrated on the images, looking for the woman's face. She had to be in here.

Yes. There she was.

He concentrated on her, his mind's eye racing back and forth over the tags in the image, committing their numbers to memory. And then she was gone. Deleted from his mind.

Cal didn't panic. He thought about the number sequences tagged in the image, knowing that any one of them might work and bring her back to him.

It was easy this time.

There she was right in front of him.

There was something important about this picture. There had to be.

Behind the image of the face a series of ones and zeroes started to run from left to right, filling in one line after another, the digits blurring as they built up over the woman's face.

At first he thought it was 1/0 code. On, off. On, off. On, off. Or maybe it was machine code, like those old games. But even as he thought that he couldn't help but wonder what old games he meant. Binary? As he wondered what the stream of ones and zeroes meant, they continued to completely cover her face and then filled every corner of his mind, his world reduced to:

```
1010101010101010101010101010101010101010101010101
0101010101010101010101010101010101010101010101010
1010101010101010101010101010101010101010101010101
0101010101010101010101010101010101010101010101010
1010101010101010101010101010101010101010101010101
0101010101010101010101010101010101010101010101010
1010101010101010101010101010101010101010101010101
0101010101010101010101010101010101010101010101010
1010101010101010101010101010101010101010101010101
0101010101010101010101010101010101010101010101010
1010101010101010101010101010101010101010101010101
0101010101010101010101010101010101010101010101010
1010101010101010101010101010101010101010101010101
0101010101010101010101010101010101010101010101010
1010101010101010101010101010101010101010101010101
0101010101010101010101010101010101010101010101010
1010101010101010101010101010101010101010101010101
0101010101010101010101010101010101010101010101010
1010101010101010101010101010101010101010101010101
0101010101010101010101010101010101010101010101010
1010101010101010101010101010101010101010101010101
0101010101010101010101010101010101010101010101010
1010101010101010101010101010101010101010101010101
0101010101010101010101010101010101010101010101010
1010101010101010101010101010101010101010101010101
0101010101010101010101010101010101010101010101010
```

1010101010101010101010101010101010101010101010101
0101010101010101010101010101010101010101010101010
1010101010101010101010101010101010101010101010101
0101010101010101010101010101010101010101010101010
1010101010101010101010101010101010101010101010101
0101010101010101010101010101010101010101010101010
1010101010101010101010101010101010101010101010101
0101010101010101010101010101010101010101010101010
1010101010101010101010101010101010101010101010101
0101010101010101010101010101010101010101010101010
1010101010101010101010101010101010101010101010101
0101010101010101010101010101010101010101010101010
0101010101010101010101010101010101010101010101010
1010101010101010101010101010101010101010101010101
0101010101010101010101010101010101010101010101010
0101010101010101010101010101010101010101010101010
1010101010101010101010101010101010101010101010101
0101010101010101010101010101010101010101010101010
1010101010101010101010101010101010101010101010101
0101010101010101010101010101010101010101010101010
1010101010101010101010101010101010101010101010101
0101010101010101010101010101010101010101010101010
1010101010101010101010101010101010101010101010101
0101010101010101010101010101010101010101010101010
1010101010101010101010101010101010101010101010101
0101010101010101010101010101010101010101010101010
1010101010101010101010101010101010101010101010101
0101010101010101010101010101010101010

And no matter what he did, he couldn't bring the woman's face
back into focus. It was gone. He wanted to weep. He wanted
to sink down inside himself and simply cease to be. He wanted
to remember something for longer than a few moments, to
hold on to it. Wasn't that how memories were supposed to

work? Otherwise how could he even begin to know himself? The thought filled him with panic. His every instinct was to thrash about, to fight his bonds, to fight a way free, but he had absolutely no control over his body.

Slowly a faint glow began to fill the spaces around the ones and zeroes, colouring them in while leaving a few spaces blank. Gradually those spaces began to form words. There were no sounds this time. The colours picked out precisely formed capital letters.

INPUT RESTART CODE

He waited, not sure what he was supposed to do. What did it mean? Had something inside him crashed? Was that what had happened? Would there be instructions for him? Would the man in the white coat fix him again?

A series of dialogue boxes took shape beneath the three words in Cal's mind. Cal focussed on them, helpless. What was he supposed to do?

INPUT RESTART CODE

Was there a series of letters he needed to put into the boxes to make a word? What kind of code was it asking for? He tried to focus on the outside world, but he could no longer see the screen; there was no man in a white coat coming to do whatever needed to be done.

INPUT RESTART CODE

The words started to flash, demanding that he do something. The longer he did nothing the more urgently they pulsed. Was it an emergency? Was something desperately wrong inside him? Was time running out?

He was sweating. Shaking.

But that was impossible. He couldn't control any of his muscles.

It was in his head, he realised. A memorised emotional trigger: fear.

But why? What did he have to be afraid of?

The man in the white coat had rebuilt him. He was safe.

Cal counted the boxes. He couldn't think of a word that would fit them.

What if it wasn't a word? What if it was numbers?

He stopped, his mind alive at the possibility. What if it was a *sequence* of numbers? What if it was *that* sequence of numbers?

Unbidden, the string of numbers that he'd been unable to get out of his head slotted themselves one at a time into the boxes.

Suddenly his head filled with images and memories, faces and emotions, the worst pains, the most delirious joys.

Second by second he came back to life.

Second by second he regained the memories that had been stolen from him.

For a moment he wasn't sure that it was *his* life, or that they were *his* memories, but as every gap inside him slowly filled with more and more of everything that made Callaghan Jones who he was, Cal *remembered*.

Then he heard a voice.

It wasn't his.

Open Your Eyes.

Chapter 19

Open Your Eyes.

The phrase filled his mind, trawling through the memories that all seemed so new. Even if this was his life, it felt like he was experiencing it for the first time. Cal wanted to whoop and holler with pure unadulterated joy and excitement, but before he could, other less happy memories rose to the fore and he wanted to weep, drowning in brand-new sorrows.

Listen to me, Cal.

Whose voice was that?

He listened hard for it, even though he knew it was inside his head.

'Who's there?'

It's me, Cal. It's your mother.

Buccaneer.

That was what they called her. The memories were still flooding back. The last few pieces of the puzzle were slotting into place as his most recent memories returned. He remembered everything, right up to the moment he sank to his knees on the steps of the Watchhouse and turned himself in.

He was a Trojan Horse. A virus in the system with access to every single piece of information Marshall Trent had ever accumulated. He remembered his mother's final instructions, how she'd planted the restart code in his brain and all he had to do was *open his eyes* – she'd find a way to be there for him. She wouldn't let him down. Not this time. And he knew that he trusted her. He would do whatever she told him to. He didn't really understand how she'd done it, but her voice would be with him, streaming into his consciousness through the Neurochip Trent's medics had inserted in his head. She'd anticipated Trent would wipe his memory and exactly how he would do it. She'd gambled that he'd become part of the machine that was the core of the *Neuralnet*, a hive mind capable of things beyond a single brain. It was just like adding processor power until you had an infinitely large computer system, each brain adding to the speed and complexity of calculation it was capable of.

She'd gambled right.

'They'll purge you of everything they don't need. They'll use you, Cal. But because we know that we can use them. Trust me.'

Even though he did, he'd been afraid he would never get himself back.

What if he forgot his dad after it being the two of them for so long? What if he forgot the mother that he'd thought dead for so many years and who he'd only just found again? What if, what if, what if? They were two powerful words buzzing around inside his head, and more frightening now that he'd found himself again.

Even now he didn't know if he was himself or some kind of back-up. Was there a difference? It was his body, they were his memories, but was it actually him? That was a philosophical question he didn't have an answer to. Right now he was just glad he could remember.

So what do I do now? he thought, hoping she could read his mind. It wasn't magic, it wasn't telepathy, it was science – the transmission of thoughts as energy, the circuitry of the Neurochip's interface translating them into words.

You don't need to do anything, not yet. Sit tight.

For how long? Dad's in here somewhere, isn't he?

I'll find him, I promise. There's going to be plenty for you to do when the time comes, Cal, believe me. But this bit I can control from where I am. You've done the hard part, now let me help you.

He could picture her and everything about the room around her. He knew exactly which chair she would be sitting in. It was the one she'd been in when she'd copied his memories. There was a bank of wires that connected her rig to the chip she'd put inside her own head. But her chip didn't work in the same way that everyone else's did. It gave her access to the *Neuralnet*, but without letting her presence be traced by the Enforcers or the spyware Trent almost certainly hid within the network to look for intruders. It meant she could do things by simply thinking about them and directly pass messages to other people if they had chips in their own heads, like now.

When he looked out through the screen into the outside world he had a better idea of where he was and what had been done to him. He leaned his head forward as far as he could, pushing against the restraint that held his forehead in place, and realised some small amount of control over his muscles had returned. No doubt it was Buccaneer's doing. He felt the restraint tug at the skin behind his ear where he was jacked into the great 'living computer' at the core of the *Neuralnet*. On the other side of the room he could see a row of white upright coffins. Each one had a viewing panel near the top.

It took Cal a moment to grasp the fact that he was looking at a row of datapods just like the one he was inside. And behind them another row. And behind them another row, and another. He hadn't understood how many there would be.

His vision was limited but he could count thirty and, given that there were at least three identical rows behind them, plus the one he was in, that meant there were 150 identical datapods in the vast room – and it was vast, he realised, looking up at the ceiling as it stretched out of sight. There could be hundreds of rows of datapods, making it an immense warehouse of data-processing power. He was right at the heart of the *Neuralnet*.

He wasn't naive enough to think this was the only room, either. *How many people does Marshall Trent have hooked into this machine?*

There was never supposed to be this many, his mother said inside his mind.

You knew about this?

I knew that it was possible, but it was only meant to be a meeting of minds, a way for a group of people to exchange ideas and work on problems. Not this . . . monstrosity. This is evil.

There was no arguing with that. *How long has it been going on?*

Too long, she said. **It will have taken years to build the infrastructure for something this large and complex. And then to populate it. You can't just grab thousands of people from the streets without them being noticed, so it takes time to find the people to feed the machine, too.**

You knew this was going on and you did nothing about it? You knew people were being snatched from their homes and brought in here to be used like this?

I didn't know exactly what they were using the technology for, Cal, believe me. And while I had my suspicions, I didn't know how they would be powering it. But I'm doing something now. I needed someone on the inside, someone Trent would put into this thing. I needed you, Cal. My Trojan Horse. I couldn't get in by myself.

The face of the woman in the picture came back to him. It was her. Did that mean Trent was using the *Neuralnet* to try to find her?

He has his spies everywhere, Cal, his mother responded.

He couldn't get used to her being able to hear his every thought.

No secrets, she said, and he was sure he heard her laughing. **I need you to keep your eyes on what is going on in the middle of the room. You're my eyes and ears. It's not only about what's going on inside the computer.**

OK, he thought, then felt a sudden surge run through his head, millions of tiny shapes in random patterns, swirling and whirring, seemingly out of control. *What's happening?*

I've put things in motion.

Put what in motion?

It's a virus, she said, intruding into his thoughts. **But this one is going to put things right. We just have to hope that it can do what it needs to before Trent gets a chance to shut it down.**

But it was too late. They had already been detected. Cal's viewing panel filled with red light that began to pulse on and off, alerting the man in the white coat who started towards Cal's datapod. The lights were flashing inside his head, too, as the defence mechanisms of the *Neuralnet* began to isolate the source of the threat. It was only a matter of time before they identified him as the source, and when they did they wouldn't just kill the virus, he realised, they'd root out its source and kill that so it couldn't propagate again.

You have to run, Cal. Now. You need to get out of there.

I can't move, he protested.

Not like that. Hide inside your mind. Go. You have to find the back door out of there. Find that and you'll be able to escape them, I promise you. Put up barriers, anything that will stop him, anything you can think of to buy a little time. It's all about time. Then she fell silent and he knew that she was gone.

She'd abandoned him? Had there been an attack on the Anarchists' headquarters?

His head exploded with tiny squares of colour, arbitrary at first, until they started quickly whirling into geometric patterns that turned and twisted. Somewhere in the distance there was a blackness that forced its way into his head, isolating part of his brain. That was Trent's virus killers, checking parts of the machine, scanning and cleaning them as they moved on in search of the source.

These blocks of colour were his defence against this blackness, his chance to get away and make his escape. He wasn't going to lose the part of him that his mother had tried so hard to keep safe.

Chapter 20

There was something out there in the blackness.

A creature?

An Enforcer?

It began to emerge slowly from the void.

There was a grey shape in the black. Gradually it grew into a shadow within a shadow, taking on shape and substance until it was more menacing than any monster. It was the unmistakable face of Marshall Trent and it was somehow inside his head.

Trent's face pushed forcefully out of the blackness. Cal tried to shove it aside and keep it back. His head was one with the computer, so surely that meant he could use the *Neuralnet* to defend himself?

Help me, he thought, and as he did so his mind instinctively triggered a simple subroutine he'd known since childhood, throwing up a fractal tree between them. Just the one, but it grew and grew and grew, each limb sprouting eight more and eight more and eight more, the branches spreading and spreading until Cal could only glimpse Trent's face through them.

One tree was never going to be enough for him to hide behind, though, he needed a forest of them. *Help me*, he thought again.

The branches of Cal's tree began to change; tiny squares of colour merged together and drifted across each other until they took on Trent's face.

One by one more of the strange fractal trees rose, branches multiplying as they strove for the digital sky. A world was being created inside his head.

Or perhaps it wasn't inside his head? Maybe what he was seeing, what he was thinking and, therefore, creating, was inside the *Neuralnet*? If so then surely it was inside the minds of every other victim of the machine who was trapped within the datapods? Did that mean each of these strange trees represented one of the minds of the others? Was that it? They were creating a forest for him to hide in, and he was the only one free to move around?

The trees twisted and changed, the colours altering through all the shades of true colour, each colour coming in 256 shades, 256 shades of red, 256 shades of green, 256 shades of blue, until there were millions of colours coruscating along the fractal branches, and finally there were thousands of versions of Marshall Trent's face, those piercing eyes searching everywhere for Cal.

Cal ran. He needed somewhere to hide. But where could he hide in a world where Trent could become the building bricks of that world and shape it to his will? So if he couldn't hide, what could he do?

His mother had told him to find the back door, but she hadn't told him where to look for it or what it looked like or how he'd recognise it if he ever found it. He needed her, but she was gone, just as she had been for so much of his life.

Cal ran. He didn't feel any physical effects, even as he sprinted far beyond what should have been his natural endurance: no aching limbs, no burning chest as he tried to breathe too fast, no stitch in his side, not even the drum of his heart beating out of control against his ribs. He could run forever here. But he couldn't outrun Marshall Trent. Here, Trent was God. He was Oden. He was Thor. He was Vishnu. He was Gaia. He was Shiva the Destroyer. He was Apollo and Hermes. He was the jackal-head Anubis and the all-seeing Horus. He was the shaper and breaker of this digital world.

'Mum!' he called out inside his head.

She didn't reply.

It brought laughter from each of Trent's faces. 'She can't help you now,' he sneered.

Trent could read his mind in here, just as his mother
had been able to. Nothing was secret, nothing at all. If it
was inside his head then Trent knew about it. But no matter
how hard he tried, he couldn't stop thinking about things,
making associations, with more and more of the truth he was
so desperate to hide coming to the front of his mind. Each
thought was something that Marshall Trent would have killed
to know. In seconds he'd betrayed the location of Buccaneer's
headquarters, the hiding places beneath the Community, how
Danni had neutralised the Neurochips, everything. He was
grateful his mother hadn't told him what her plans had been.

'Ah, so she didn't trust you then? Kept you in the
dark. Clever woman. But then she always was.' Trent's
mocking laughter rang out from every mouth, drowning
the digital world in sound. There was no delay, no moment
of consideration as he digested the information. Trent had
laughed the moment the thought had crossed Cal's mind.
'There's no hiding from me, boy. You should have worked
that out by now, Cal. You might as well throw yourself upon
my mercy, because I will find you. I won't hurt you. It's your
mother I want. You can help me. I might even forgive you if
you do.'

Cal didn't believe him. He was going to run. He'd always
intended to run. And now his life depended on it. His, his
mother's, his father's, maybe even Sasha's.

'Don't worry, I know all about the foolish games my
daughter has been playing. She will learn her lesson eventually.
It's about choices, no matter how misguided, and the effects
they have. When she sees the impact of her actions, she'll
understand, and she'll turn her back on you, boy, because we're
blood. Blood is thicker than any youthful idealism. It pumps
through our veins. It's a little bit of me inside her. We're the
same, no matter what she thinks right now. Just like you and

your mother. You can't help yourself. I understand that. It's not your fault. It's genetically hardwired into you.'

Again the intrusion. Cal tried to block his thoughts off, build a wall that he could hide his mind behind, but nothing would keep Trent out.

He had to find the back door.

As long as he was trapped inside the *Neuralnet* there was no hope. Trent would purge his mind, properly this time, but only after he'd picked it clean of everything that might be of use to him in his fight against the Anarchists. Then Cal would be gone forever.

He continued to weave in and out of the fractal trees that were yet to change, knowing it was only a matter of time before Trent took control of their datapods.

'Come out and play now, old friend,' Trent said.

Cal had no intention of stopping. He would keep running and hiding until there was nowhere left to run, no place left to hide.

All around him the fractal trees were transforming faster and faster until Marshall Trent's face surrounded him. 'Time to come out of the boy,' Trent goaded, and Cal realised he was taunting Buccaneer.

Chapter 21

Cal felt the change rather than saw or heard it.

It took him a moment to realise that his mother hadn't abandoned him at all.

She had been biding her time, waiting to reveal herself, knowing that Trent would capture him.

The data stream that represented her presence inside his head poured out into the neural computer that only existed within the consciousness of those trapped within the pods. She began to take form. There was no mistaking that it was her, though her avatar looked younger and fitter than she had in real life. Did Cal look different in here? Were their avatars something that lay between the truth and how they wanted to be?

'I'm here, Trent. Let my son go. We both know that it's me that you want, not him.'

'Indeed I do, Buccaneer. That is what I'm supposed to call you, isn't it?'

'Names don't matter in here,' she said.

A thousand of Trent's faces split with a smile. It was the same beneficent look Cal had seen looking down from the infoscreens for his entire life. That smile was calculated to reassure the onlookers that he was only ever doing the best for everyone, and that they had nothing to fear, he would keep their enemy at bay. They could trust him, because he loved them all. But Cal's eyes were wide open now. He knew it had been nothing but lies and deception. Marshall Trent's smile was as fake as his news broadcasts.

The face changed suddenly. A torrent of data slid from each of the fractal trees, running down into a rippling pool of tiny colourful swirling number sequences and coding lines that gradually merged, turning, twisting and taking shape. Marshall Trent, bigger, stronger, fitter and much younger than he was in real life, emerged from the pool to stand in front of them.

'Let my son go,' she insisted again.

Even though Trent had taken on a different form, his response was the same: laughter. Why should I? Give me one good reason. You see, even without his memories, he is still valuable to me.'

'Run, Cal. Let me deal with Trent.'

'No . . . I can't . . .'

'Remember, if I don't make it out of here, I still love you. I've never stopped loving you.'

'How touching,' Marshall Trent said.

A flash of lightening filled the infinite space.

Cal paused for a moment, unable to move, despite how much he wanted to start running again. She hadn't abandoned him. How could he abandon her? She'd put herself between them, even though Trent was so much bigger than her, but what could he do to help her in a place like this?

And what would happen if he was hurt in here? It only existed in the mind . . . so would he be hurt in the real world? The implications of that thought started to run through his mind and Cal realised exactly what she was trying to tell him. *If I don't make it out . . .* If she died in here, then there would be nothing left to go back to her body; her body would just be left there, empty, sitting alone in that chair and slowly rotting.

Marshall Trent pushed her out of the way with little more than a flick from the back of his massive hand. She fell to the ground, but was up again quickly. *'Run!'* she yelled at Cal again, but even before the word was out of her mouth Trent hit her again. This time the blow was much harder. It sent her skidding into one of the towering fractal trees the dictator was yet to infest.

The colours shifted and changed at her touch, leeching them of blues and greens. She shook herself and clambered back to her feet, but Cal could see that there was something wrong with her.

Part of her face had changed. Her features weren't as distinctly formed as they had been. Her cheek and lower lip were wrong. It was as if she couldn't keep it all together. Trent was going to destroy her one little piece at a time.

Cal couldn't leave her there, but there was nothing he could do to help. He turned, only to walk into another of the trees.

Vines and branches whipped out from it, wrapping themselves round him and holding him tight. They pressed his back against the digitally constructed trunk. Tighter and tighter they wound, and the more desperately he struggled to free himself the tighter the branches constricted, drawing him into the tree.

He felt sheer agonising pain, even though he knew that it couldn't be real. *It's just a computer,* he thought. *It's not real. It's just a computer.*

Trent lashed out again, striking Buccaneer's face with such force it snapped back with a sickening crack. It was a hammer-blow. Her body went limp and she fell like a puppet whose strings had been cut.

She sprawled on the ground with her head at an unnatural angle, her legs folded up beneath her. She wasn't moving. She didn't seem to be breathing – could she even breathe inside the machine?

Slowly, no more than the tiniest fraction at a time, she began to fade. Her features became less distinct. Her arms began to merge with her body as if she was just a single shape barely held together.

'Mum!' Cal screamed, as what was left of his mother's avatar became transparent and she faded away to nothing.

He could only hope that Danni or Sasha was with her. Maybe they'd pulled her out of the machine before Trent could kill her inside it? But even if they couldn't he didn't want to think about her dying alone. She'd sacrificed herself to save him. He couldn't let that be in vain, but what could he do?

'What indeed?' Marshall Trent's mocking laughter filled the digital world.

Chapter 22

'So it's just you and me now, Cal,' Trent said. 'You don't mind if I call you Cal, do you? It feels like we're old friends. We've been through so much together.'

Cal struggled to fight back tears as grief and anger warred inside him. He wanted to beat Trent to a bloody pulp, but he couldn't do it, not here, and not back in the real world, either. He couldn't bring down Marshall Trent with brute strength – he was so much bigger than him in both places. He was going to have to use his wits.

'Oh, Cal, do you really think you are cleverer than me? That's disappointing.'

For a moment Cal had forgotten that Trent could look inside his head; the shock of his mother's slow fade into nothing had thrown him off guard. He'd let his defences slip. Cal tried to rebuild the mental wall, but he couldn't get beyond a few bricks before he remembered her and then she was all that he could think about.

'I didn't say that,' Cal said.

'You didn't have to.' Trent smiled. 'It doesn't have to end this way, though. Remember, your father's still here. Did you want to save him? You still can.'

He felt a pang of regret as he realised he'd barely given his father a second thought while he had been caught up in this world, despite the fact that it was because of him that he was there.

Trent waved his hand towards the space where only a few minutes before his mother had stood trying to defend him, trying to buy him the time to escape that he'd wasted. 'You're a bright kid –' he began.

'I'm not a kid. Not any more. You've seen to that,' Cal snapped.

'There's a place for you here. With me.'

'Why would I want to be with you? You killed my mother and you're holding my father hostage.'

'Because you, Cal, hold the key to all this. You're the one person who could help broker peace with the Anarchists. And, whether you believe it or not, that is all I have ever wanted. Peace.'

'Why would anyone listen to me?'

'Isn't that obvious?' Trent said. 'Because you are the son of Buccaneer. You're her flesh and blood. That makes you a symbol to them. They'll listen to you. They'll worship you if you let them.' He let Cal think about that for a moment, before saying, 'She used to work with me. Did you know that? We wouldn't have any of this without her.'

'Liar!' Cal screamed, but he knew it was true. His mother had admitted that she'd invented the Neurochip, and without the chip there would be no *Neuralnet*, and without that no datapods and no prisoners linked brain to brain.

'And no peace, don't forget that,' Trent said, finishing his thought, though Cal knew that what he *really* meant was that without the chip he would never have been able to keep such an iron grip on power for so long.

'That is true, too,' Trent conceded. 'We understand each other. So join me, and be part of the future. All you have to do is confess. Let me into every dark corner of your mind, every recollection, let me see and hear everything you know about the Anarchists, and I will see that you are rewarded. But more importantly I will see to it personally that your father is set free. That's what you want, isn't it? All you have to do is tell me everything you know, and everything you don't even know you know.'

'How can I tell you what I don't know?'

'Just let me into your mind.'

Which meant there had to be places inside his mind that Trent couldn't root around in already. Trent didn't have the key to unlock them. Not yet.

'You catch on fast. Like I said, you're a bright kid.'

'What will you do to the Anarchists?'

'I will offer them the chance to repent, to announce publicly that they were in the wrong – some may have to serve a punishment for the public good, but they will not be harmed. You have my word.'

'And those who refuse, what about them?'

Trent didn't answer straight away. He didn't need to. Cal knew what he would do: they would be wiped and put into datapods like the one he was in, used to power the machine and monitor the people of New Edgehill, looking for anomalies, for faces that didn't fit, for plots and conspiracies. In other words they would be turned on their own.

It wasn't a lucky guess, he realised. Somehow Trent's thoughts had fed back into his own . . . he'd been able to read his mind in the same way Marshall Trent read his.

That was unexpected. However it had happened, it changed everything.

The vines holding him lost their iron grip, falling away. Trent began to fade. And one after another the trees returned to the vast palette of colours they had been before Marshall Trent had possessed them.

A moment later, Cal was looking through the viewscreen of his datapod while the man in the white coat tapped on it to gain his attention. Behind him Cal saw the unmistakable figure of Marshall Trent making his way towards him.

Air hissed as pneumatic clasps released the locks that kept the datapod sealed. He tasted the change in the air even before the front had completely swung open, freeing him.

The man in the white coat worked on the buckles restraining Cal. 'So, what do you think about my offer?' Marshall Trent asked Cal.

Trent's skin was grey and waxy. He looked tired. Really tired. Had possessing the *Neuralnet* drained him of energy? It was possible. Cal's head felt heavy as the strap was released, his arms and legs weak.

'How long have I been in there?' Cal asked the man in the white coat, ignoring Trent's question. He could barely stand unsupported as the man helped him out of the pod.

The man glanced at Trent before answering. 'Six days.'

Six days? Cal couldn't believe it. How could he have been in there for so long? It didn't feel like six days. But how could he tell? He'd spent so much time with no memory, with no concept of time, no concept of self, just those pictures constantly streaming through his mind. He'd lost six days of his life.

The man in the white coat offered him a forced smile. 'Do you know what your name is?'

'Of course I do.'

The man raised an eyebrow. 'And it is?'

'Callaghan Jones.'

'How . . .?' The man in the white coat turned to Trent. 'He had the mind wipe. We did all the tests. There was nothing left of him in there.'

'He had help,' Trent explained. 'I'm not sure how she did it, but I know who. She was the best.'

Was . . . Cal's heart sank. It was so much worse hearing it here, worse than witnessing it first-hand. Hearing the word 'was' made it real.

'Who?' the technician asked.

'His mother,' Trent said, clearly unwilling to give away any more than that. He turned his focus on Cal, ignoring the man. 'So, my offer? I need an answer, Cal.'

'I don't have a lot of choice, do I?'

The alternatives were worse than he could imagine. He knew that if he went through with the brain wipe there would be no bringing him back this time, no rebooting his memory to restore him. He'd simply cease to be. There'd be no one around to help him this time. Trent would get the information that he wanted. He wouldn't be able to stop that from happening. No matter how hard he fought, it would only buy him a few hours, a few days – in other words nothing.

He did have a choice, though. He could watch, study the technician and work out a way to escape.

Chapter 23

The room they gave him was smaller than the one he had at home, but it was warm and clean, and they brought him meals at regular intervals. It was clinical, the floor covered with wipe-clean tiles for practical purposes. The bed offered a view of the window, which itself showed only sky.

He was a long way up.

The man in the white coat was called Kit. Despite appearances, he was less than ten years older than Cal. Cal had all sorts of questions he wanted to ask him, but he'd seen the way Kit looked at Trent. Kit wasn't an ally in the making. He was terrified of Marshall Trent. There was no way he would cross him or even risk upsetting him. He would report everything Cal did and said back to the dictator.

Cal had to keep his guard up, so he pretended that everything was fine. It wasn't easy, given everything that had happened inside the machine, but it was the only way he was going to get out of there. So he lied as if his life depended on it, which in way it did, and kept a happy smile plastered on his face.

For three days he barely got out of bed, and never unassisted. At first it was because he was simply too weak to stand for any period of time, let alone walk, but it soon became obvious that they were prepared to wait while he recuperated, however long that might take. Of course the longer it took, the longer they had to wait to do whatever it was they had planned to do with him, so Cal was in no hurry to get better. One thing was for sure: it wasn't going to be a simple interrogation. They wouldn't simply ask questions about the Anarchists; they wanted to get inside his head. That way they'd know whether what he said was the truth, the whole truth and nothing but the truth. It wasn't only that they'd be able to root around in there to find secrets, it was that they'd know any kind of lie he tried to offer before it had even taken shape in his mind.

Not that Cal was a good liar anyway.

Trent promised the procedure wouldn't damage him, but could he believe him? This was the man who had killed his mother in front of him. He'd never forget the crunching sound of the hammer-blow as Trent struck her down. He couldn't trust the man after that. But he didn't need to. All Cal needed to do was learn what he could from him and use it to his advantage. To do that he needed to delay the inevitable moment when they finally got inside his head to get at the secrets they thought were in there.

By the fourth day he was on his feet and able to move around the room, but as far as his captors were concerned he was still a long way from regaining his strength. He feigned weakness whenever Kit came into his room. It wasn't difficult because it was impossible to tell the difference between fever sweat and the sweat of exercise. So while Cal built up his strength with press-ups, squat thrusts and shadow boxing, his overseers thought he was bed-ridden.

'How long does it take people to recover from the datapods?' Cal asked Kit, beads of sweat tracking lines down his temple. It had been close this time. The technician had come into the room less than a minute after he'd finished a particularly gruelling set of exercises.

'No one has ever come out of there before,' Kit admitted.

'No one? You mean they stay in there *forever*?' He almost said until they died, but stopped himself because he didn't know if they would ever truly die or if the machine would keep them on some sort of basic life-support, which was worse.

'Not while I've been here. You're special, Cal. The fact you even remember who you are is a miracle. I don't know how you did that. But it's not my job to know; I just keep an eye on the units and raise the alarm if something goes wrong. No one has ever woken up. Once someone goes in, they stop being people in the way we understand and become part of something so much greater.'

'The *Neuralnet*?'

Kit nodded. Did that mean they stopped being living things when they went inside the datapods? 'Mister Trent has told me to keep you comfortable,' Kit continued, 'to see to your needs and do anything I can to aid in your recovery, so if there's anything you need let me know. When you're strong enough he'll want to sweep your mind, but he doesn't want to risk damaging you. Like I said, you're special, Cal.'

'I think I need to sleep some more,' Cal said.

There were any number of things he could ask for, and he might even get them, including time with his dad, but it was vital he maintained the pretence of weakness if he was going to avoid being hooked up to the machine again. He had to give himself as much time to think as he could. This was a battle of wits now, and that meant he needed information.

There were different ways he could collect that information. One was reconnaissance. He needed to get out of his room, even if it was only an escorted outing in a wheelchair. He needed to see what was happening beyond these four walls. He couldn't just walk out of the building. And he wouldn't get far in a hospital gown even if he tried. Trent would have armed guards on the main door to make sure that didn't happen. Cal hadn't heard the servo hiss of any Enforcers patrolling the corridors, though. Whenever the door opened he paid attention. He was trying to hear two things: people beyond the door and the tell-tale sound of a lock disengaging. He heard neither.

This time when Kit left his room, Cal slipped out of the bed and checked the door. He tried the handle tentatively, expecting an alarm to sound. The door offered no resistance as he opened it a crack. That was all he needed to see Kit's white coat as he walked away down the corridor. Cal eased the door closed again and counted to a hundred in his head, listening all the while. Then he opened the door again.

The corridor was deserted. Cal decided it was time to venture out.

Apart from Kit, Marshall Trent was the only other person he'd seen since emerging from the pod. Were they the only ones here? Well, not the only ones, obviously there were hundreds of poor souls crammed into the datapods.

He heard footsteps coming along the corridor. It was too soon for Kit to return unless he had forgotten something.

Cal turned quickly, the door clicking closed behind him, and dived back on to the bed, barely managing to pull the covers over him before the door opened.

It was Marshall Trent. 'Hello, Callaghan. How are you feeling this morning? Fit for the fight?'

'Tired,' Cal said.

'Understandably, but you're on the mend. We'll have you up and about in no time. I'm sure you're eager to help me, aren't you?'

'Of course.' It was one small mercy that they weren't hooked up to the *Neuralnet* together or Trent would have known he was lying through his clenched teeth. At least this way he had a chance of fooling the dictator, but as soon as Trent realised he was lying any pretence at working together would be forgotten.

'Another day then,' Trent said. It was a statement rather than a question and Cal found himself nodding. Another day sounded good.

'Can I ask you something?'

'We're friends. You can ask me anything.'

'Can I see my dad?'

Marshall Trent inclined his head slightly, seeming to think about it before refusing his request. 'Once we've got this all sorted. But right now my primary concern is your health. You're weak. You don't need the stress. You need to rest. Your father is fine. Trust me.'

Cal couldn't argue that he was strong enough, because that would mean he was strong enough to face Marshall Trent's questions. All he could do was nod his agreement and say, 'Thank you.' Perhaps he was a better liar than he'd thought because Marshall Trent offered him a slight smile and said, 'I'll leave you to it then.'

Cal lay there until Trent left.

He needed to be calm if he was going to escape.

He needed to have his wits about him.

He couldn't let anger or fear get the better of him.

When Cal opened the door the next time he made sure the corridor was clear before he took a deep breath and ventured out.

He'd done his best to memorise the way back to the datapods, but he needed to know what else was nearby, and how it could be used to his advantage, before he found the way out. Cal turned in the opposite direction to the vast room of datapods – where he knew Kit would be monitoring the prisoners of the machine – placing each footstep softly, careful to avoid making a sound.

There were half a dozen other doors on the corridor, all of them on the same side.

He tried each one in turn. The first couple were locked.

The third clicked open and his heart started to race. He pushed it open slowly, suddenly sure he was about to find Marshall Trent waiting for him on the other side.

Instead he found a room identical to his own in every way. The bed had been slept in and worn clothes had been thrown over the back of a chair in the corner. There was a photograph beside the bed of a young man and an older couple. This was Kit's room. He didn't have time to investigate it, though. Not yet. But he'd come back. Maybe there'd be a security pass or something he could use to help get out of the building?

Cal slipped back out into the corridor and silently closed the door behind him.

The next door was locked, too. So Cal felt a moment of anticipation when he reached the final door. He pressed his hands against it and willed it to open on to something that might help him.

It was locked. And then it wasn't. He didn't know how it happened, but there was a soft click of the lock disengaging and the door pushed open. He looked about for security cameras or some other way for someone to be watching him, but couldn't see any obvious lenses hidden in the corridor. Could his mum have opened it somehow? Was that just wishful thinking? That snap after the hammer-blow had sounded so final. Was Trent watching, leading him into a trap?

The room was dominated by the familiar shape of a leather chair identical to the pilot's chair his mother had used in the Anarchists' command room. But before he could even set foot inside he heard Kit's voice at the far end of the corridor.

He was caught in no-man's-land, torn between stepping inside and closing the door behind him and trying to sneak back to his room without being caught.

Kit came round the far end of the corridor, his attention on the rig in his hand, recording some observation or checking the readings from one of the datapods.

He walked with his head down, deep in conversation with someone on his rig.

Cal took a gamble and tried to sneak back to his own room. He was halfway down the corridor when Kit ended his call and looked up to see Cal.

'Kit,' Cal said, then slumped against the wall, sliding slowly to the floor as the technician rushed to his side.

'What are you doing out of bed?' Kit said in surprise.

'I thought . . . it might . . . help,' Cal lied, deliberately
struggling with the words. 'I wanted to see how far I could walk.'

'OK, well, let's get you back to bed,' Kit said, stooping
to help him stand, and with Cal leaning heavily on him they
walked back to his room. Kit seemed to have bought his lie.

'I just want to be strong for Mister Trent tomorrow,' Cal
explained.

Kit passed him a glass of water and waited until Cal had
drunk most of its contents and sunk back into the pillows,
seemingly exhausted from his little adventure. 'I'll let you get
some rest,' Kit said and left him alone again.

Cal's heart was still racing when the door closed.

Chapter 24

He waited until after Kit's next visit to check up on him before he risked venturing out of the room again. He was beginning to think of it as every bit as much of a prison as the datapod.

Kit placed a tray of food on the cabinet beside his bed quietly because he didn't want to wake Cal, who was pretending to be asleep.

Cal waited until he was gone and then counted slowly to a hundred, giving Kit time to move away down the corridor before easing himself out of bed. He waited behind the closed door for another minute, listening until he was as sure as he could be that the corridor was clear, then he opened the door and slipped out, and still in his hospital gown, hurried back to the room with the console at the far end.

The heavy door was unlocked, so Kit hadn't ratted him out to Trent. He stepped inside and closed the door behind him.

He'd hoped that he would be able to lock it from the inside, so that should anyone come looking for him he'd have a chance of using the machine to engineer a way out of the Watchhouse before they could drag him out of the chair. But there was no lock. He wedged a chair up against the handle instead. It wouldn't stop a determined shove, but it ought to buy him a few extra seconds, and that might be all the time he needed.

Cal climbed into the leather chair and pulled the headset down over his head. A glass visor dropped down over his eyes. There was a small viewscreen built into it that glowed into life. A prompt came up for a password. Without it he wasn't getting into the system, but what would Marshall Trent have used? People normally picked combinations of words and numbers that meant something to them: pet names, wives, husbands, important dates, anniversaries. They were predictable. But he didn't know Marshall Trent so how was he supposed to even

begin to guess what might be significant to the man? And if he
got it wrong what would the consequences be? Cal shuddered
to think.

But there was one phrase his mother had been drumming
into his head over and over. Open Your Eyes. Could it be that
simple? He whispered it softly, pronouncing each word carefully,
and watched the letters form on the screen. 'Open Your Eyes.'

He was in.

He smiled. It was obvious that Buccaneer had engineered a
hack to let him into Marshall Trent's system.

Cal found himself in the same forest of fractal trees, each of
them moving and shifting, and changing colour as they detected
his presence. All he had to do was find what his mother had
planted: the failsafe that would shut the whole thing down.
She'd said that Trent hadn't known about the back door, and
wouldn't know what it was even if he stumbled across it. He
tried to think. She'd warned that the program was capable of
changing its appearance, but that no matter what shape it took
he would always be able to recognise it.

Not that he would have long to. The system would identify
him as an intruder and deploy defences, and if it considered him
a threat to its continued existence, it would terminate him with
its virus killers. So he had to work fast and hope that he could
find what he was looking for before he triggered any of the no
doubt many traps Marshall Trent had put in place to protect his
empire and the single greatest source of his power. It was clear
that his mother had believed that without the *Neuralnet* there
was every chance Trent's empire would crumble. But for now it
felt as if Cal couldn't see the wood for fractal trees.

He needed to think. Where would she hide it? What did he
know about her that might provide him with a clue?

The truth was very little. She was a mystery to him, this
woman who had given birth to him and then abandoned him to

become Buccaneer. How was he supposed to predict what she'd do or how she'd think? Just because they were related didn't mean he could read her mind.

He moved closer to one of the trees, examining the string of data that swirled round its trunk, and the branches that reached up into the digital sky. There was nothing that stood out immediately as different or out of place among the links to all those minds in the datapods, so perhaps he had to find his way through the fractal forest and out the other side into whatever lay beyond the trees?

He didn't have long in here: either the machine would sense his invasion or someone would find his body back in the real world, so he ran for his life, weaving in and out of the weird forest that was forever changing around him. He fought his way through tendrils of fractal branches that reached out into the spaces between the trunks. He wriggled and he squirmed and he ducked, desperate to avoid coming into contact with any of them. If they touched him, it would be enough to trigger the alarm.

The air crackled with electricity. Sparks leaped from tree to tree as information passed from one datapod to another back in the real world. Cal was sure that that hadn't happened the last time he'd been here, but what did it mean? It took him a moment to realise what was different. The last time he'd been part of the *Neuralnet* – or in essence he'd been one of the trees, one of the energy sources in a datapod. This time, from the chair, he was in control of this digital world. That was why he saw things differently. That was how Marshall Trent had been able to make his face appear in place of each and every tree. He'd been in this chair, running command lines to shape the landscape.

Cal paused for a moment, suddenly and surely lost. He had no idea where he was trying to run to, and was horribly sure that the world kept reforming itself around him and that he

wasn't moving at all, never mind in the wrong direction. There
had to be a better way to negotiate the fractal forest.

Open Your Eyes.

His mother had hacked into the system and used her chair
as a means of becoming one with the neural interface, he knew
that much. She hadn't been inside one of the pods. Everything
she'd done, she'd done from the outside. He needed to think
like her. He needed to remember he was an outsider here. He
wasn't just a stream of data surging round an energy core. He
was different. What did he know for sure? She'd planted the
failsafe a long time ago. It was there, and all she needed to do
was trigger it, but she couldn't do that alone. She'd given her
life trying to defend him rather than locating the failsafe and
maybe saving a lot more people. What did that mean? Was it
just a mother's love? Or was it something more?

Think! Open Your Eyes!

His indecision resulted in one of the tendrils of trailing vine
reaching out and touching him. Cal felt a spark jump between
them, then another and another as the vine tried to coil itself
round him. He backed away from it quickly, almost into the
next fractal tree behind him, but felt the same surge of energy
jump across from another tree to the next and the next until
it closed in on him and he felt a sudden surge as energy jolted
through him, making every hair on his body stand on end. He
gasped, crying out as more and more of the vines coiled and
writhed round him, trying to drag him down.

Cal panicked, lurching away from the nearest vines, but
didn't manage to break the connection. Instead more of the
trees made contact with him. He felt an incredible rush of
power race through his system as a flood of information filled
his mind. In an instant he felt as if he knew everything there was
to know. Everything. He was connected to it. He felt it swarm
inside him. He felt his body swell with it, growing and growing

as if it would never stop, until he stood there like a giant in the digital landscape of the *Neuralnet*.

All the personal details of the people trapped in the datapods – their ages, original names, their PIDs, their supposed crimes – came flooding into his mind. So many of them had been swept up by Enforcers and taken off the streets, presumed dead or simply disappeared, and here was the proof. Not that he could share it with anyone now that his mother was gone, he thought bleakly. He was alone in this fight now. He'd inherited it from her. They needed him, even if they didn't know who he was.

By connecting to the datapods he was able to access the information stored in their minds. It was overwhelming. Cal struggled to cope with the constant outpouring of data, trying to sift through it for something that might help him find the failsafe. This was his one chance, he realised, while he was wired up to the machine like this nothing was secret from him. He needed to dump all the information he could into his brain, pull down everything he could possibly learn while he was still connected to the *Neuralnet* and then get out of there, destroying it in the process if he could.

He thought of his own time in the pod and of his mother's picture and how it had kept coming up in his searches over and over again. He had tried so hard to burn it into his memory for fear he'd never be able to recall it, that the image came instantly to mind now. Seeing her, even like this, was enough to spur him on. He hoped he'd never forget this picture of her now, no matter what else happened.

Somewhere lights flashed, sparks flew and energy surged through the trees, leaping from branch to branch before arching down into him. He knew what was happening. The people trapped in the datapods had found him. Now they were all focussing their attention on him – or rather to a task that Cal didn't even realise that he had given them. Each of the pods sent him snippets of data – pictures of his mother, information about the invention of the Neurochip, details of the creation of the *Neuralnet* – but none of it was helping him locate the failsafe. They continued their search, trawling through the infinite soup of their memories to produce anything that might be connected.

There was so much of it, but nothing seemed relevant. His mother had been good at hiding her presence from the machine, but not as good as she thought. The people in the pods had thousands of images of her stored away, hundreds of articles about her work, and then he reached the stuff about her death and the lies he'd always believed.

He sifted through the information as it came in. It took him a moment to understand that none of it, not a single byte of data, connected his mother with the Anarchists.

What did that mean? Was the machine ignorant of the fact that she was – had been – Buccaneer? No. That was in here. This was something else. This was about Anna Jones, its creator. This new data spread across the fractal trees like wildfire. They snapped and crackled with raw energy as they worked to process it, then something changed. A darkness crept through the trees, filling the spaces between them. Some kind of defence had been tripped. Time was running out. The system knew that it had been breached. And that meant that Marshall Trent knew, too.

The images kept changing. He saw two distinct sets of things, one that represented his mother and another that was associated with Buccaneer. They flew by so quickly that he was unable grasp most of them. So much of what he was learning meant nothing to him; it was just a store, batches of data collected and then stockpiled in a dark corner of the machine's memory, forgotten. He chased it all down, thinking that the darkest corners were exactly where he was most likely to find his answers.

His own mind wasn't capable of processing all this information quickly enough, but with the aid of so many datapods working on the problem together he finally found something that connected the two. A single reference point.

The blackness crowded in, running through everything like an ever-growing oil slick oozing into every space. When it touched one of the strange pillars of writhing colour, it drained everything from it until the fractal tree withered and crumbled. In his head Cal heard a sigh and then felt the absence of something that had been there a moment before. Did that mean the connection had simply been broken or had something much worse happened to the inhabitant of the pod? He moved away from the darkness, running through the trees, his arms outstretched, fingers trailing against trunk and branch and vine, desperate to keep ahead of the dark and knowing that every step he took meant sacrificing others to it.

He wasn't worried about connecting with the trees. Instead of trying to restrain him the vines moved aside to let him through, the neural pathways closing just as quickly behind him. The forest was helping him.

At last the flickering images of the amassed data about his mother and Buccaneer stopped. They came together on a single image. Cal found himself looking at a picture of his mother holding a small child. He hadn't seen the picture before. It was him. In the background there was a ship; an old fashioned sailing ship. The ship flew the black flag of the Anarchists.

What did it mean? Was this what he'd been looking for?

The fractal trees swayed as if a breeze pushed through their boughs, gently at first, this way then that, and with each movement he saw hundreds of shapes he'd not yet connected with. What was causing the cyberwind? Was it a virus come to crush him? More data surging through the *Neuralnet*, pouring out of the hidden minds that formed it? There were so many more datapods that were out of his reach. What secrets did they hold?

Trent would know how to find out, but Cal wasn't Marshall Trent. He was discovering things more by accident than design, but he was being driven in one particular direction, he was sure of that.

One tree stood straight and tall, unbending no matter how fiercely the cyberwinds blew.

A glance at the blackness told him it was multiplying all around him, engulfing the fractal forest. Soon the digital world would be black, all the lights and colours snuffed out.

Cal ran.

There was nothing that he could do to slow the progress of the security program, but that didn't mean the others couldn't help him. And that was exactly what they seemed to be doing. Did that mean the people trapped in the datapods could still think for themselves to some extent, even if their minds had been wiped? He tried not to think about it as he ran. He focussed on the single unmoving point up ahead and ran.

It was only when he drew nearer that he realised what he was running towards. It wasn't a tree at all. It was tall and needle-straight as it pierced the digital sky. A flagpole.

As he reached it something started to form at its base. For one sickening second he thought it was the blackness, but then a simple black shape slowly unfurled and started to rise upwards. A black flag. The flag of the Anarchists.

His mother had built a Black Flag program into the core of the *Neuralnet*.

Chapter 25

'Time to go,' Buccaneer said.

She'd been sitting in her rig-chair for hours, visor down over her eyes, scanning the uplinks and downlinks for the tell-tale pulse of data that would say the time was right. She was utterly exhausted. The physical demands of maintaining the connection were slowly sucking the life out of her. But that was the nature of the *Neuralnet* now that Marshall Trent had subverted its original purpose. This should have been so good for people. A coming together of minds. The essence of what a society ought to be. Instead he'd turned it into a nightmare.

'A trained monkey could start the broadcast. I want to do something *useful*,' Sasha complained.

'I need you to do this, Sasha. It's important. It could be the most important single act that happens today. I'm trusting you. It might not feel that way, but I am. Be ready to start the broadcast. Everyone needs to know the truth. Now is the time. It's in your hands.'

Sasha shook her head. 'I don't want to argue with you, honestly, but I still don't understand why you had to send Cal in there. My father will purge him. There'll be nothing of him left.' She paused, thinking. 'Why risk him if you can access the *Neuralnet* from here?' That was the question she'd been wanting to ask from the beginning. She'd resisted asking it for as long as she could, but she needed to know.

'Just because I can enter the machine from here doesn't mean I can control it the way I could from inside. There are things I can't do from out here. I'm limited to being an observer. I can distract, I can learn, but I can't actually *do* anything to affect or alter the architecture of the system. He's got measures in place to stop me doing that. Are you ready?'

There was no point in arguing. It wouldn't change anything. She nodded.

She had seen the film they were going to broadcast on the old laptop. She wasn't entirely sure what difference it would make. Even if they could tap into the vast processing power of the *Neuralnet* and have it seen on every infoscreen in every Community across the Isles, even if every Citizen in the Reunited Kingdom stopped what they were doing in order to watch it, all Marshall Trent had to do was tell them it was more Anarchist lies and they'd swallow his explanation whole, wouldn't they? They were conditioned to believe him. Breaking that conditioning wasn't going to be easy while their Neurochips were plugged into the net.

But whenever she questioned Buccaneer all she said was, 'Trust me. Now is our time.'

'What about Danni?'

'She'll be ready to do her part,' Buccaneer said, with no mention of what part that might be.

Danni had taken Sasha over the route a couple of times so she was familiar with the subterranean twists and turns of the old buried city. She'd be able to move about New Edgehill unseen, out of the prying sensors of her father's Enforcers and cloud-skimming Drones. She ducked from building to building, tunnel to tunnel, moving fast. The clock was ticking its merciless countdown. She couldn't slow down or stop to catch her breath. She needed to be in place when Buccaneer called upon her. She wouldn't let her down. She was one of them.

Marshall Trent had made the mistake of underestimating his daughter.

It was a complicated passage. She'd wanted to set down markers – splashes of paint on the walls perhaps – to ensure she didn't take a wrong turn, but Danni had been adamant she commit it to memory. There couldn't be a single clue to her whereabouts, and certainly not a gingerbread trail that could be followed all the way back to the Anarchists' headquarters.

The journey covered almost twice the distance it would have if she'd been moving above ground. At last, she reached the foundations of one of the towering SPUs. She emerged from the subterranean world into a tangle of cables beneath one of the massive infoscreens and sank back against the concrete wall, gasping for breath, and stayed there in the darkness, before firing up the laptop.

She worked quickly, without light, her hands connecting the cables as Danni had shown her. The hours of practice, repeating the connections over and over again until she could do them blindfolded, paid off. She plugged the laptop into the loop that led to the network of screens all across New Edgehill.

She sat there, alone in the dark, finger poised over the enter key.

No matter what happened next, the world was about to change.

She pressed the button and waited. In less than a heartbeat, all the screens across the Isles burst into life.

'Citizens . . .'

Chapter 26

Open Your Eyes.

The message burst into every single chip connected to the *Neuralnet*, the single imperative exploding into the minds of the Citizens. It was on every single infoscreen in New Edgehill. And it was on the glass of Cal's viewscreen visor. The same message flashed up everywhere. Even though he wasn't hooked up to the *Neuralnet* any more, his own chip pulsed with the same message, creating a feedback loop of sight and sound. He was still in the system and could still see the fractal forest, but he was aware of the room his body was in outside it. One layer of reality on top of another.

Open Your Eyes.

In the streets people stood bewildered. They all knew something had fundamentally changed, but didn't understand what, so they stood there lost in confusion, waiting for someone to explain. All Cal could think was that the three-word phrase was built into the Neurochips, and when he'd triggered the Black Flag program it had broadcast directly to them, triggering the change they'd been designed to cause. Sparks flew across synaptic bridges, closing off the connections where Trent had previously been able to exert influence and control. Right up until that second these people had never known what true freedom was, now suddenly they did, even if they had no idea what to do with it.

'Citizens.' The single word brought the infoscreens to life. Out of habit people looked up to see whatever it was Marshall Trent wanted to show them.

Cal watched intently as the image appeared on his own screen. When the image finally formed it wasn't Marshall Trent looking down on them. It was his mother! It was Buccaneer! In his confusion, he hadn't registered that it wasn't the dictator's voice he'd heard.

She'd survived. Somehow, she'd survived.

A sense of euphoria swept over Cal. His mother was alive!

'Citizens,' she repeated, 'when you look up here at these screens you expect to hear the truth. You expect to hear of the war on the eastern front and the threat of the Anarchists and how Marshall Trent only loves and wants to protect you. Today, for the first time, these screens really will tell you the truth, and this is it: you have been lied to. For a generation you have heard lies and let them rule your lives. You have made decisions for the future, important decisions, for your families and the ones you love, based on these lies, because the truth has been hidden from you. Now it is time that you open your eyes.'

The viewscreen changed to show some of the images that Cal had seen on the old laptop, including the faked footage of the dead and wounded in battle, as well as, finally, the film set of the Exploratory Outpost bombing, which had supposedly happened in Bright Town.

'We are not at war.'

Buccaneer let that sink in.

'We haven't been at war with anyone other than ourselves for years. That is the truth Marshall Trent never wanted you to know. It suited him for you to believe that we were. While you were all afraid of a distant enemy, and the promise that they could arrive on our shores at any moment, you weren't worried about what was going on at home: the austerity measures, the homeless disappearing from the streets, his Enforcer Drones policing our every move. You even let him inside your head!'

There were muttered voices of agreement, confusion and dissention, as the Citizens of New Edgehill and every other city across the Isles struggled to understand and accept what they were seeing. It was a message none of them wanted to believe. Cal could understand that. He wanted to pull the visor off, clamber out of the chair and run down to the streets and yell,

'It's true!' But they wouldn't believe him any more than they believed her. She was Buccaneer, head of the Anarchists, a well-known enemy of the state. Why would they?

It left Cal feeling absolutely useless. He had access to the immense processing power of this living, breathing computer, and no idea how to use it to actually *help* spread the truth Marshall Trent was so desperate to hide.

As he watched the feed from the various screens he realised that this was *exactly* the same footage he'd seen on the laptop. She wasn't talking to the world live. But that didn't mean she was dead, did it?

Cal couldn't help it. He feared the worst again.

The images became more rapid, flashing with blinding speed as they imprinted subliminal messages on the minds of those watching. The Anarchists were using Marshall Trent's own techniques to free the people he'd held in thrall for so long, hammering the truth of their message home while they stared up at the big screens. By the time they stopped watching they'd not only know the truth, they'd *believe* it.

The datapods burst into life, answering the sudden surge in demand for information as people tapped into the *Neuralnet* to find out the truth.

The black ooze had stopped moving, but a significant portion of the forest of minds had already turned grey and lifeless. Cal approached the nearest of the active data streams and reached out to touch it, dipping his hands – his avatar's hands – into the tidal flow of information. Instead of disrupting the flow he simply let it wash over him, savouring the thrill of it as it coursed through him. There was so much power here. It was incredible. Dizzying. Cal tried to focus on it, to tap into the constant flood as the images and lines of code that called them up, the search strings and the command lines drowned his mind. He felt as though he were spying on everyone all at once, everyone who accessed the system, everyone who wanted to know the truth for themselves.

Sparks swirled everywhere, climbing up his body to swarm around his head in a vortex of raw processing power, and there, in the heart of it all, he saw Marshall Trent.

Cal pulled his hand free of the data stream, breaking the connection as quickly as he'd made it. Had Trent seen him?

But if Trent was in the system . . . did that mean he didn't need the chair to access it? Did he have another way of operating the *Neuralnet*?

Chapter 27

That single instant of connection had been enough to fill Cal's mind with Trent's intentions, even if he couldn't filter them immediately. So much had come flooding into his brain that he struggled to cope with it and not lose all sense of himself beneath it. Information poured into him like a torrent. Compared to the vastness of the living computer he was *nothing*. He had no way of controlling it. He could barely hold it at bay.

Trent was issuing instructions to his Enforcers. And Cal could understand every word of those missives.

Trent was ordering them to find and neutralise someone quickly and silently. He was mobilising every Enforcer at his command, calling in reinforcements from outside New Edgehill. His quarry wasn't going to escape him. *Let them hide like rats in their stinking lair, I will flush them out . . .* Those thoughts weren't Cal's, they'd bled into his mind straight from Marshall Trent's, dripping with hatred. From the number of orders being dispatched near simultaneously, there must have been hundreds of Drones streaming in from outlying areas as far away as Bright Town and Oaks Ford.

Cal's heart surged with hope.

There was only one person Trent could be so determined to stop, and he'd been there, he'd slain her avatar, but he was still mustering every weapon at his disposal to bring Buccaneer down. That had to mean she was alive, didn't it?

The minds trapped within the datapods dispatched the dictator's orders, sending Enforcers to every place she'd ever been sighted – including the ones Marshall Trent had learned from Cal. There was nothing he could do about it, but it still sickened him to think that he'd betrayed her when he should have been running for his life, while she'd risked everything to buy him the precious seconds he needed to escape. He recognised some of the places the Enforcers were being sent to: the SPUs out on the edge of his Community, the infoscreen with the hidden entrance beneath it, even the submarine-style hatch that led down into the underground bunker where Buccaneer's headquarters were. And it was all his fault. All of it. He'd betrayed them because he was a stupid child.

Data streams calculated the vectors for possible locations. Cal was sure he could hear the Drones being dispatched, even from in here. They'd scour the area, ready to drop their incendiary devices and wipe out entire Communities if it meant they got Buccaneer. They wouldn't hesitate. There was no human 'moment' when they'd think about what they were about to do. They were machines. They obeyed the codes fed to them, following orders.

They would find her, even if it meant bombing the hell out of those Communities Trent knew were sympathetic to Buccaneer and the Anarchists. And when they found her, they would kill her.

Marshall Trent was on the edge of losing everything. He was a wounded animal backed into a corner. That was the most dangerous kind. Cal needed to do something. He was the only one who might be able to help her. He needed to make a difference. But what?

Open Your Eyes.

Where was he? How could he access the Enforcers' orders? He was inside the system. That was the answer to both questions. So if he could access their orders, could he *change* them? Perhaps there was some way he could infiltrate the data flow and misdirect the Drones? But if he did that he'd have to find a way to hide it from Trent, otherwise the dictator would understand he had a ghost in his machine. The moment he realised the *Neuralnet* had been infiltrated it would be over. He'd storm into the room at the end of the corridor and wrench him out of the system. Or worse. No. Cal needed to find another way. The problem was he couldn't even leave the building so how was he supposed to help?

Cal's mind raced with possibilities. He needed to stay connected to the net for as long as possible. He had to know everything that was happening as it happened, that was the only way he was going to be able to affect the outcome, even if it was just to give a warning seconds before it was too late to make a difference.

But right now it was imperative he didn't give himself away. For the time being at least, she was alone out there.

Somewhere in the *Neuralnet*, a datapod interpreted his unspoken question as a request for information. He hadn't even realised he'd given the command, and as a map of the plaza came to life all he could think was he'd just given himself away. But he hadn't. The map showed a moving dot, tagging it Marshall Trent. Cal smiled, amazed yet again by the power at his disposal.

New Edgehill was the most watched over city in the entire kingdom, with thousands upon thousands of surveillance cameras spying on every corner of the city. For once, he was grateful for Marshall Trent's paranoia.

The dictator was out in the open and on the move. He wasn't rushing. In fact, he showed no signs of urgency.

He was on foot, Cal realised. Where was he heading? Was he still in contact with the net? Had his chip been destroyed by the Black Flag program Cal had triggered? Did he even have a chip?

Vector analysis projects that target is heading towards transport depot. Target has not been assigned a chip and is not currently connected to the *Neuralnet*.

Not connected. And not only that, but Marshall Trent wasn't heading in his direction.

He had time – even if only a little – to try to figure out what to do. It was interesting to know that Trent had never had a chip fitted, so how did he gain access?

Marshall Trent accesses the *Neuralnet* with the aid of an adapted rig.

Can he still be tracked? Cal wondered.

The position of Marshall Trent is always monitored in case of any security issues. He must be protected at all times.

Am I a security issue?

You are protected by the Black Flag.

If Trent wasn't connected to the *Neuralnet*, then the risk of discovery was reduced. If the machine could warn him as Marshall Trent reconnected – he didn't get to finish the thought before the machine interrupted:

An alert will be sent when Marshall Trent comes online.

Chapter 28

And then it hit him: it didn't mean his mother was alive at all . . . Just because Trent was sending out the Enforcers didn't mean he was hunting Buccaneer, it meant he was hunting whoever put the footage online, and if it wasn't auto-uploaded by the Black Flag program there was only one other person foolish enough to go up against Marshall Trent like this: Sasha.

If it was Sasha, being Trent's daughter wouldn't help her, not this time. She'd gone too far for a slap on the wrist.

Cal was thinking on his feet. He wouldn't be able to reach her – whichever her it was – in time. He wasn't even sure he'd be able to divert the Drones without giving the game away, but Trent wasn't online, so he had a window of opportunity, no matter how small it was. Now he had to use it.

Could he use the *Neuralnet* to locate Sasha? That would be a start, especially if it turned out she was back at the Anarchists' headquarters. He'd be able to warn her. But surely Trent had tried that?

Then something else struck Cal: what if Buccaneer's Black Flag had destroyed every Neurochip it pulsed through? What if that's what 'Open Your Eyes' meant? Maybe that's why they weren't uplinked? No, Cal reasoned, thinking it through. He'd experienced the searches executed by people out there after Buccaneer's message had broadcast, so that couldn't be right.

Sasha Trent is not connected to the net.

Maybe not, but could he track her using her rig, like the machine could track her father? It made sense. She was the one who'd been obsessed about being tracked through his rig when they were down by the river what seemed like a lifetime ago.

Sasha Trent does not have a rig registered to her.

Another dead end. He felt like screaming. *What about her last-known position? Can you calculate that?* he thought.

Immediately the image superimposed on his visor showed the Watchhouse in the plaza where he'd surrendered himself over a week ago. Did that mean she was still here? When?

The answer was instantaneous.

The last-known sighting of Sasha Trent was nine days ago with suspected Anarchist Callaghan Jones.

Which left two possibilities: one, she'd been captured, or, two, she'd been able to hide and stay hidden. Sasha was good; she could move around New Edgehill without being followed. She knew exactly how Marshall Trent's digital eyes and ears worked. If anyone could hide from them, it was her. If she'd been captured, there would be records in here. So he had to assume she was out there running. And now that he'd triggered the Black Flag, Cal had no way of reaching her.

It was all guess work. But Trent was guessing too. The only difference was he had more watchers out in the city. But maybe Cal could turn that to his advantage, too?

Thinking fast, he ran through the possibilities. There was no guarantee Sasha was broadcasting from the Anarchists' headquarters. In fact, it was highly unlikely. She was smart. She'd know the source of the signal could be traced, so even if she had uploaded it there, she'd be on the move already. Even from his limited time there, Cal knew there were plenty of places in that labyrinthine network of underground tunnels that she could be sheltering in. It made sense for them to keep out of sight of prying eyes, and he was sure they'd kept him away from plenty of safe houses in case something had gone wrong.

His surrender had been a high-risk strategy. He'd willingly turned himself in to the enemy. When he thought about it he realised how few Anarchists he'd actually met: Sasha, Danni and his own mother. Three people taking on the might of an empire? Surely that couldn't be the extent of the resistance. His mother must have known Trent would scour his mind for every last detail, including their names and faces, so there had to be places in the underground network he didn't know about. But could he work out where they were? Could the machine reverse-engineer probable locations based on what he knew?

What do you know?

He asked the question, and in response felt himself being pulled forcefully towards awareness – he felt the clammy leather of the chair against his skin, saw streams of information scrolling across the glass of the visor's viewscreen, even the towering fractal trees mutated into something more *real*. Real people. In the forest of the network, Buccaneer's Black Flag virus was doing so much more than simply rendering Neurochips ineffective. The black ooze that had been slowly creeping through the digital landscape had retreated. Obviously, he was no longer an enemy. Or rather, next to the Black Flag he was no longer an enemy worth worrying about. The system was under an entirely different kind of attack now.

Cyberdust flew from the flag as it flapped in the cyberwind, tiny fragments of data strings leaking out of the core. They shouldn't exist outside the trees. The trees themselves were bright with constantly changing colours. Wherever the dust came into contact with the environment it caused a corrosive reaction. The stuff of the digital world lost its shape and its vitality. Instead of turning black as the trees had when the ooze had crept up their trunks, the landscape was bleached of all pigment where the dust fell. Speck by speck it glowed a pale yellow before burning out. Seconds after the dust fall everything was silent. The datapods were being lost to the machine. Soon there would be no *Neuralnet*.

Once a tree had absorbed the dust and undergone its moment of transformation, it produced its own black flag like a single flower at the top of its stem and released more of the tiny fragments of corrosive black data into the system.

The virus was growing stronger, and spreading at an alarming rate. It wouldn't take long given its current growth before it shut down the whole network. And that was a double-edged sword. Cal needed *Neuralnet* to work to his advantage.

Without it he didn't stand a chance against Marshall Trent.

Without it he couldn't help Sasha or Danni.

Without it he couldn't help his mother – if she could be helped.

Without it he couldn't help himself.

Chapter 29

Cal was enthralled by the coruscating colours as the trees were drained of knowledge and information. So much information lost forever.

Or did the living computer have a back-up? That's how his mother had saved him, after all, wasn't it?

The machine was working, but did it have enough processing power left to help him, given it was already working against him, scouring the images stored in its memory banks in search of correlations, cross-references and points of symmetry? When it found them, it sent out the Enforcer Drones to capture, or maybe even kill, anyone that had crossed Marshall Trent. The Anarchists' rebellion would be crushed.

That, Cal realised, feeling sick, was the sole purpose of this incredible piece of technology: to track and control the Citizens of the Isles. But it was capable of so much more than that. He'd seen that in just the short while he'd been connected to the machine. There were answers in here, without doubt, answers to big questions. With all this brain power, surely the ability to defeat mental and physical disease was there, the ability to harness infinite eco-friendly power, to nurture dying species, to just make life *better* . . . It was all there, in the machine, wasn't it?

A society must be judged on how it treats its weakest members.

The message had come from the machine. Somewhere deep down inside, it knew what was right. It wasn't an unthinking machine like the Enforcers who just followed orders. Because at its core the *Neuralnet* was human, wasn't it?

Yes. We are.

He tried to put himself in Marshall Trent's shoes. What would he use the machine to keep track of? This time there were no answers from the system, no responses to point him in the right direction. Perhaps the question was too vague? Or perhaps the machine had already lost too much of its capability to answer?

Show me a list of identified Anarchists, Cal thought.

The request returned a rapid result as streams of data scrolled in front of him: pictures of people of all ages, each of them stamped with a single word 'REASSIGNED'. There were hundreds of people. Thousands.

Reassigned? Reassigned to what?

Insufficient data.

The first name in the list was James Durant. The name didn't mean anything to him, but since he had the most powerful computer in the world at his fingertips, if there was anything worth knowing about him it had to be stashed somewhere in its memory banks, didn't it?

Tell me about James Durant. Everything you know.

Again, the system reeled through a long list of files that contained everything it had on the man. There was nothing that wasn't less than five years old. It was as if he'd simply disappeared. Or died.

Show me James Durant's death certificate.

There is no death certificate issued to James Durant.

There wouldn't be, would there, if James Durant had found his way inside one of the datapods?

No.

If there was so much information in the system about Durant, then what about Sasha? The thought was out there before he could stop it.

Files and references started to roll again, some of them were no more than folders containing pictures of her. Others were more interesting. He glanced through them quickly, catching glimpses of a couple of them together, images captured by CCTV. He had been completely oblivious to the fact that they had been under surveillance, but the way she looked up towards the camera in a couple of them meant she had been all too aware of their prying eyes.

The only thing the images proved was that Sasha Trent and Callaghan Jones were connected.

One picture seemed out of place. A single shot of him alone. It was a few years old. Certainly from before they'd ever met. What was it doing in here? Had it been filed away by mistake?

Sasha Trent and Callaghan Jones are connected.

He tried other folders, other files, and while much of the material was related to her activities within the Anarchists and links to Buccaneer, it didn't shed any light on where she might be hiding now. He found her academic records. Clearly Sasha had excelled in school, but that came as no surprise. Right from the beginning he had known that the girl was ferociously intelligent.

The last folder in the digital register was marked Birth Records.

It was empty. Had Buccaneer's virus destroyed the contents?
No.

Had someone deleted the files? Why would someone delete her birth certificate unless they had something to hide?
Information protected.

Chapter 30

That caught Cal by surprise. It wasn't the response he had expected.

'Protected' was different from insufficient data. That meant the truth was in there, but he couldn't get at it. There had to be a way to circumvent whatever protection Trent had put in place. And that meant it had to be a secret worth protecting. Part of him knew that knowing Sasha's secret – because that was what it was, after all, not Marshall Trent's – was an invasion of trust and a betrayal of their friendship. Maybe they just hadn't had long enough together, he reasoned. Maybe she would have told him sooner or later?

But another part of him couldn't help but wonder what if she didn't know? It didn't matter that it might have no bearing on what he was trying to do, but it was a straw and he was desperate enough to clutch at any straw he could find right now. He knew how computers worked. They hid system files. Anything that governed the way a machine worked was hidden so users couldn't accidentally delete or corrupt them. So maybe a seemingly empty folder wasn't empty at all?

Showing hidden files? It couldn't be that easy, could it?

In less than a heartbeat a series of files glowed into life but lacked any kind of preview function, so it was impossible to see even a hint of what was inside them.

Access denied.

More security. Layer upon layer of it. Marshall Trent was determined to keep this secret. What made no sense to Cal was why, when the living computer was full of so many more damning activities she'd been guilty of with the Anarchists, proof of her birth was so difficult to find?

It didn't make any sense. *Why hide it? And who had access to these files? Just Marshall Trent?*

Registered users, Marshall Trent and . . .

Cal watched the second name appear on his viewscreen, unable to understand what he was being told. Two users were attached to the files. Two people who could access Sasha's secret. Trent and his mother.

Why would she have access to information about Sasha? Why hadn't Trent taken her access away?

Insufficient data.

Of course. It wasn't like the system was going to betray its custodians. Maybe it was something to do with the fact his mother had created the Neurochip, and by extension the *Neuralnet*. Did she have automatic access to all the data that streamed through the pods?

No.

If he could get into the files maybe that'd be different, but – **Password-protected content. Password required.** – he wasn't getting in.

Trent had almost certainly got alarms set up, too. Even if he was offline that didn't mean the *Neuralnet* didn't have ways to warn him. It could send a pulse out to his rig, telling him to jack into the hive mind. It could tell him that someone like Cal was close to learning his deepest, darkest secrets. And if it could do that . . . who knows what else the machine was capable of? *The Black Flag virus may be eating up terabytes of data per second and shutting down datapods, but would it attack security protocols first or even differentiate them from the rest of the system?*

Security protocols are in place.

Well, that answered that. But without the password he wasn't getting in.

Cal had no idea what form the password took; was it a word, a phrase, a series of numbers or letters? Was it possible to hack it? The only phrase that stuck in his head was the one that had unlocked the chips: Open Your Eyes.

Password incorrect. Access denied.

How many more attempts would he have before it shut him out? He had to be careful what he thought. The problem was that now he knew there was a secret, its simple existence was already gnawing away at him. That was the thing with secrets, they had a way of taking over.

Password-protected content. Password required.

It was pointless.

He had to move on. He was wasting time. The Black Flag virus was corrupting and digesting the data held in the system. If his mother had wanted him to access this stuff, she should have given him the key. She knew what was in that deleted file, after all. If it was important surely she'd have given him a means to access it.

He remembered the one thing that had been imprinted on his brain, even when there was nothing else there, when all his memories had been scrubbed clean. One thing, a string of numbers. He hadn't been able to get them out of his head.

The numbers came unbidden just as he had known they would.

Access denied.

He'd been sure it was going to work.

He needed to think. How do you break into a secure system?

He could hack it, or at least try and hack it, but it was always better if you had the password.

There must have been thousands of passwords. Millions of combinations. Billions! Would the system hold a record of them all? Surely not, all he had to do was think it and quickly!

File of all encrypted passwords being processed.
File now available for download.

The file was vast. Every single encrypted password stored by the system, a huge list of common passwords used in the New World in the last 10 years, including Marshall Trent's and, more importantly, his mother's secure encrypted password. Now it was a case of looking for a needle in a digital haystack. Thankfully, that's precisely what dictionary searches were made for.

He was now only a few seconds away.

Access granted.

The files opened up in front of him.

Chapter 31

There were no obvious secrets in the file.

Cal wasn't sure what he'd expected to find, or why his mother should have access to it.

The file showed Sasha's date and place of birth. She was a little older than he'd assumed but that meant nothing. She had never told him how old she was.

Other hidden files included reports from school teachers, attendance records that showed that she'd never missed a day, and test results which only reinforced how intelligent she was. There was nothing out of the ordinary, but he carried on looking until he found a simple medical statement. It was only one line. Sasha had succumbed to a disease that had meant she could no longer attend school. And then it stopped. There was nothing else in the file.

Why hadn't she returned once she'd got better?

But . . . she had . . . hadn't she? There were other records, not in these hidden files. He'd read them in the open files. So why hadn't Trent tried to keep them secret, too?

Cal checked back. There was a gap of several years before Sasha had resumed her schooling. It seemed that she'd picked up exactly where she had left off.

He read the date again and again. There was something significant about it, but he couldn't see it. There was something about it he should remember. He'd only been young at the time . . .

A list of events raced through his mind as the machine searched the datapods for every noteworthy reference it could find for it. Most of them meant little to him, but time and time again references appeared linking the date to the creation of the first Neurochips, their mass production and their insertion into the Citizens' heads and the creation of the *Neuralnet*.

And then he remembered what was important about that date. It was the year his mother had walked out of his life.

It didn't matter how many facts spooled though his mind, none of them matched the importance of his mother's disappearance, the creation of the Neurochips, and Sasha and the secret Marshall Trent had tried to bury. But how did they all fit together?

Cal returned to the hidden file, rereading the last few entries again. There was a word he'd missed. It changed everything. *Succumbed*. He'd assumed it meant contracted on first reading.

Incorrect definition.

Succumb: to fail to resist pressure, temptation, or some other negative force. Yield. Give up. Surrender. Die.

And that was it. The secret. Sasha Trent had not returned to school because she had succumbed to an illness.

Sasha Trent had died.

But, if that was the case, who was Sasha?

Chapter 32

Sasha was in trouble.

Images of her running came up on the glass of his visor. He had no idea where they were originating from. That would have been too easy. His first thought was the machine was tapping into the surveillance cameras out in the Communities. It made sense. That was what they were for. But these weren't coming from a static camera. He realised what that meant: these were coming through the lens of a Drone. She'd been found by an Enforcer. He was watching her run for her life.

Numbers flowed beneath the image – kilometres, metres, centimetres, millimetres, counting down with alarming speed. The Drone was almost a kilometre from the target – Sasha – even if the camera made it appear as though it was in touching distance. It was capable of shooting, with deadly accuracy, from this range.

Cal didn't recognise the area. Sasha was above ground, dodging between buildings. The Drone was looking down on Sasha, tracking her as she turned left and right. It painted cross hairs upon her back, as she paused, gasping for breath, before ducking inside a building. The Drone didn't stop, it hovered, drawing closer to the rooftop, switching over to thermal imagery to locate her within the building. It didn't even need to wait for her to come out from hiding.

There might be a way down to the tunnels in there, but there was no guarantee. The Drone continued to circle.

Sasha's heat signal didn't disappear. She was cornered. No way out. The Drone was waiting on the kill order. A red light started to flash at the bottom of the screen. **Target acquired.**

Don't fire, please, please, please don't fire . . .

The flashing light began to slow down. **Standing down.**

Cal released the breath he hadn't even realised he'd been holding and watched the cross hairs change from blazing red to white, disengaging. Somehow he'd overridden the Drone's command structure.

It's not her, he thought, lying and desperately hoping the Drone's command system wouldn't be able to tell the difference. *It's not who you're looking for. Leave this Community now. Go. That's an order.*

The Drone started moving again. For a moment he thought he'd done it, but then he saw Sasha come racing out of the other side of the building. The Drone's cameras swivelled, and it launched itself after her. He sensed rather than saw or heard the Drone's summons as it sent the call out to every Enforcer in Marshall Trent's New Model Army. Along with her coordinates, the message included her projected vector, factoring in a human attempt to randomise her route, and all the known Anarchist hotspots in the vicinity. There was nowhere she could hide. It had eyes everywhere and she was alone out there.

Sasha clambered over the debris clogging up the passageways between buildings. The Drone followed her, tracking her from an ever-decreasing distance.

Cal started to recognise a few of the buildings. It was the angle that had thrown him. She wasn't far from the SPUs and the entrance into the tunnels. If she could get that far she had a chance. But she wasn't moving fast enough.

They were closing in on her. The Drone's proximity sensors indicated four more incoming.

He couldn't help her from where he was. He couldn't defend her.

Defensive mode adopted.

The image turned and shifted, scanning the skies. The cross hairs fixed upon the first of the Drones streaking through the sky towards Sasha. Three more black shapes grew in the background behind it. He had control of the first Drone. She wasn't alone any more. He could fight for her. As soon as the thought crossed his mind the response came: **Arming weapons.**

The nearest of the Drones exploded, a gout of flame filling the air a split-second before debris crashed to the roof of a building below. The black shapes grew in size, approaching rapidly, only for another to burst into flame as Cal's Drone shot it down.

Messages streamed across the Drone's head-up display.

Choke point identified.

Concealed enemy position.

Threat isolated.

Under attack.

The Drone's sensors had picked up on more of its kind incoming, weapons primed. It moved quickly, racing directly towards the centre of the choke point it had identified, where all of them came together, closing the distance before they were able to bring it down.

Self-destruct initiated.

There was nothing else the Drone could do to protect her. It was sacrificing itself to take out as many of the Drones as possible. That was the best it could do for her now.

The screen turned red. Then black. It stopped broadcasting. The signal dropped. It was gone.

He reached out for another one, trying to take control of it, but there was nothing. He didn't know if that meant the last Drone was down, or if they'd found a way to keep him out. It didn't make any difference. Sasha was on her own now. Cal could only hope he'd bought her the time she needed.

Chapter 33

They were coming.

Sasha knew the sound of a Drone. It was unmistakable. And getting closer.

The video file had been uploaded to the infoscreens, and now it was out there, playing in an endless loop. She'd done her job. Now she needed to get out of there. She couldn't go back the way she'd come; it would take too long. She needed to move fast. She couldn't afford to waste the time. Not now. Now it was happening. Every second counted.

She knew where she was. She could cut through the Community and pick up one of the tunnels on the other side. It wasn't going to be the shortest route, but it offered the least exposure. She'd need a little bit of luck, but the risk was worth the time it saved. It had to be. She needed to get back to Buccaneer.

Her escape route cut between buildings, skirting some of the infoscreens that dominated this part of the Community. There were plenty of Citizens out on the streets, lost. She could understand the look of utter confusion on their faces. Their world had just been turned upside-down. Their eyes had been opened. Now they were waiting for someone to tell them what to do. That someone was Marshall Trent. He always told them what to do. But he wasn't coming to save them this time. That more than anything else proved that everything they'd ever been told was a lie. So they turned to each other, but no one was ready to tell them what to do. Sasha felt sorry for them. She wanted to tell them what they should be doing: storm the Watchhouses of the man who'd spent his life lying to them.

But that wasn't her role in the uprising. She was under strict instructions to get back to Buccaneer. She cast a fretful glance behind her, up at the sky. The Drone was closing in. There were more black smears in the sky behind it. There was more than one of them up there. Her father had scrambled an entire squadron, she realised, feeling sick. He wasn't playing this time. Even if he knew it was her, that wasn't going to change a thing. She was a problem that needed sorting out.

Sasha pushed through the press of bodies, forcing a way through. She needed to move faster. These people were slowing her down with their confusion. Some moved aside willingly, but others didn't, becoming a barrier.

Sasha didn't risk another backwards glance.

She had her eyes on one of the old warehouses up ahead.

It was one of theirs. The spray-painted circle over the square of the Anarchists tagged it.

Gritting her teeth, she ran on, every muscle in her legs screaming.

She crossed the wide open space between streets as part of a wall in front her exploded in a shower of dust and shattered stone and veered left, zigzagging as more shots missed their mark.

The warehouse doors were less than a hundred metres away, but they might as well have been a hundred miles.

There was no way she could cross that much open ground without one of the Drones picking her off.

But there was nowhere left for her to run.

She was in the Drone's cross hairs. She could *feel* it. It would take out the entire building, the entire street, if it had to. Expecting to feel a sudden explosive pain and the world to come to an end – or at least her part in it – Sasha sprinted out into the open.

The pain didn't come.

No more explosions. No more whistling shots flying over her head.

She dived inside the building, knowing that there was a flight of iron stairs that would take her down into the subterranean network. She saw them across the vast empty space of the abandoned factory floor. Sasha ran for them, and clanged into the darkness below.

She heard movement in the room above her, heard the hiss of an Enforcer's servos, and panicked, pushing a heavy door closed behind her. She needed to brace it with something. Anything that would keep the Enforcers out. But without a light she was in trouble. She fumbled around for broken bits of timber and rods of metal from the disused machines, and jammed everything she could get her hands on behind the door. It wouldn't stop an Enforcer and she knew it.

Sasha stumbled across the dark floor, trusting her memory that there was another door on the far side.

Halfway across, she fell, and cursed the sudden stab of pain in her knees as she landed. She bit off the cry when she heard banging on the other side of the door. They were out there. She pushed herself back to her feet and started moving again tentatively, disoriented in the dark. She reached the wall and felt her way along it, trying to find the door. As her hand closed round the handle, she tugged and it opened. As she closed it behind her an explosion tore at the building above.

The Enforcers had blown the first door wide open. She had to move. Now.

There was another flight of stairs. She climbed them, panicking when she hit a trapdoor. She hammered at the wooden boards until they gave way, and clambered out into the light. Sasha recognised the entrance to Buccaneer's headquarters. She was here. She'd done it. But she'd brought the Enforcers to their door.

Chapter 34

The computer was almost dead.

The last remnant of life would be disconnected soon. In seconds. Almost all the once vibrant data spikes were no more than a sickly yellow beacon burning slowly down to nothing. The fractal trees had given their black bloom to the data stream. There was nothing to be gained by staying inside the *Neuralnet* any longer. He couldn't be sure that Sasha had made it back to the Anarchists' headquarters, but he hoped she had. He was sure now that it was either her or Danni who'd triggered the broadcast, not his mother.

Cal opened his eyes and breathed deeply. It was almost over.

He removed the headset. The disconnection left the *Neuralnet* near silent. All he could do now was try to get to Sasha.

He looked around, amazed at how far he'd come dressed in nothing but a hospital gown. Anarchy flowed in his veins. *Maybe I really was born for this,* he thought, pushing himself out of the chair, which had moulded itself to his body. He padded over towards the door and listened. The corridor beyond was quiet.

Cal opened the door and made his way along the corridor as silently as possible, banking on the fact that Kit would be going insane trying to stop the inevitable collapse of the *Neuralnet* and the damage the Black Flag program was doing to the disconnected datapods. What he hoped was happening was that they were waking up and opening their eyes like the rest of New Edgehill and the Isles. What he feared was happening was that they were flatlining one after another.

Cal paused at the last door, the one that opened into the vast warehouse of datapods, and looked through the small observation window in it. His fears were coming true. Kit rushed from one to the next without a clue of how to help them or stop what was happening.

A stairwell took Cal down eight flights of stairs to the world outside. Eight flights. Eight vast spaces filled to overflowing with datapods and prisoners waking up.

He reached the street level, expecting the building to be on lockdown, but since so much of the Watchhouse had been controlled by the living computer, without it Marshall Trent's order was descending into chaos. Cal stumbled outside, not caring how he was dressed.

Halfway down the steps, he slowed down. All around him people were wandering about aimlessly. Without their Neurochips they didn't know what they were supposed to be doing. Whereas before the good law-fearing Citizens had kept away from the smooth marble of the plaza they were now standing in the middle of it, aimlessly turning in circles. There was nothing sacred about this place any more.

Cal tried to think. To plan. He wouldn't be able to get to the Anarchists' headquarters, even if all the Enforcers were focussed on Sasha and Buccaneer, especially now that he didn't have the machine to protect him. His only hope was to find another way in, but the Enforcers that hadn't been drawn into the suicide bomb up above his old Community would be watching every entrance he knew about, and more he didn't. But he had to try. Anything was better than doing nothing.

He crossed the plaza lost in thought, only for someone to yell, 'Cal!' and grab his arm. He tried to resist as they pulled him into a doorway. There were no lights on inside, but the door was open and they tumbled through it. He saw her short cropped blue hair first. Danni. He grabbed her.

'Easy soldier,' she said, crawling out from under him. Then she seemed to realise just how little he was wearing under his hospital gown, and turned away, blushing.

'We've got to help Sasha. She's in trouble.'

That made her turn round again. 'How do you know?'

'I saw it . . . through the *Neuralnet* before it went down. Enforcers are after her.'

'Do you know where she is?'

'At Buccaneer's headquarters. Where you took me.'

'Why would she go back there? That wasn't part of the plan.'

'It doesn't matter, does it? That's where she is.' He focussed on the fact that Sasha needed him, needed both of them. Everything else could wait. 'Now can we stop talking about it and do something to help her? Ladies first,' he said, smoothing down his hospital gown.

He had no idea if Buccaneer had shared her plan with Danni, or if, as with him, it had been a need-to-know thing, with layers of secrets to protect her from Marshall Trent should it all go wrong.

She nodded and set off, but instead of going back out to the plaza she moved deeper into the building. There was row upon row of canned produce stacked high and deep in aisles. What there weren't were customers or a shopkeeper. 'This way,' she said and within a few moments she was ushering him through a door that led to a cellar.

'How can this even be here? An Anarchist hideaway right beside Marshall Trent's Watchhouse?' The audacity of it was incredible. It was genius. You wouldn't expect the enemy to be living in the house next door. Cal was struck by the irony. Marshall Trent had always preached about familiar enemies, and here they were living right beside him. *If only he'd opened his eyes,* Cal thought, having to stifle the laugh he felt rising.

'All these buildings were built on top of others. Nothing's really new. Just because this is New Edgehill and they tried to bury *old* Edgehill, doesn't mean Edgehill simply disappeared. The foundations of the old town were still strong. It was easier to incorporate the new buildings on to the old than it was to clear the area. It's like patching a piece of software. You put build two on top of build one; you don't start again when there's no need to. This will have been street level once upon a time. There are still entire streets down here, a city beneath the city.'

Which certainly explained how Sasha was able to disappear so easily, and move from Community to Community unseen.

Danni turned on a lantern. Litter and debris had been pushed to the edges of the cellar, creating a path from one side to the other. There was another door ahead of them. They moved from cellar to cellar, and then into tunnels that joined one space to the next. Only of course now he could see they weren't tunnels at all, they were streets that had been covered over when Marshall Trent had buried the old city to start anew. He felt the same sense of disorientation as the first time he negotiated this subterranean world, when the girls had led him down into the safe house.

'Will this get us close to Sasha?'

'Just about all the way, but it hasn't been used for a long time.'

'Why didn't she come this way? Why risk the streets? It doesn't make sense.'

'Buccaneer never told her about these underground roads.'

'Why not?'

'Not my place to say, but I don't think she really trusted her. You get that, right? You've spent time with her . . . There's something that's not quite right.'

'You think she's a spy for her father?'

Danni shook her head. 'No. Well . . . no. But . . . Buccaneer only let her into the headquarters itself recently. Before that she's always been kept at arm's length. Better to be careful, I guess.'

That made sense. He couldn't shake the feeling that Trent would do to his daughter what he'd threatened to do to Cal. If the information he needed was in her head, he'd have taken it. That was the kind of man Marshall Trent was. He had to get to her first. He had to help her.

'This is it,' Danni said at last.

Ahead of them was an old brick wall. There was nothing remarkable about it. Like the rest of the tunnels it was in a poor state of repair. There was a dark patch where damp was seeping through from the other side, and it looked like the roots of a tree had found their way down, beginning the process of reclaiming this part of the tunnel for nature. What there wasn't was an obvious way of getting through it.

The lantern played the wall's length, revealing a series of metal pegs that had been driven between the mortar, making a ladder of sorts.

'Just watch what I do, and do the same. Don't think about it, that only makes it worse,' Danni said, handing him the lantern.

'Great. No thinking. I can do that.'

'I know you can. That's why I like you.'

She moved deliberately up the wall, giving him time to make sure he understood the sequence of moves she was making, so he could duplicate them, and then at the top, reached up to the roof and pushed at a concealed trapdoor. Light came flooding into the underground street, along with a shower of dust.

Cal blinked against the sudden brightness.

'Turn it off,' Danni whispered.

He fumbled with the lantern's switch until it fell dark.

'Leave it down there,' she added.

He wasn't going to argue with her. If things went well they wouldn't be coming back this way. If things went wrong, they wouldn't be coming back at all.

'Cal?'

'Yes?'

'I'm glad you came back . . . you know.'

'Me too.'

'Would have been boring without you around.'

Chapter 35

The Enforcer didn't move to stop Sasha; it didn't need to. There was nothing she could do.

Buccaneer was dead.

Sasha couldn't stop her tears. She couldn't be dead. She couldn't. Sasha wouldn't let that happen. She pounded on Buccaneer's chest, willing her back to life. It didn't help. Buccaneer still lay slumped in the chair, the headset caught in her hair.

Had she done it? Had Buccaneer finished her mission or had it all been for nothing?

The Enforcer moved.

Just a twitch. A servos hiss as its head turned. No more.

Sasha stepped back in panic, expecting a jolt of electricity to bring her down, but the Enforcer showed no sign of threatening her. Instead it stopped in front of Buccaneer's body.

'Beyond repair,' it said.

Beyond repair. What a strange way of expressing that the woman was dead. So distant. So inhumane. But then, it was a robot.

Sasha was about to surrender when it struck her: what if Cal was still trying to make contact? What if he was waiting for her help? He was alone in there. He was depending on them. She needed to let him know what had happened, and warn him that Enforcers had breached the headquarters. He mustn't come here. He had to run.

She removed Buccaneer's headset and held the limp body close to her own, trying to lift her out of the chair, but she barely moved. From somewhere Sasha found extra strength, giving everything she had, and lifted the body, but she couldn't hold it for long. Buccaneer's body slipped from her grip. It was all she could do to stop it from hitting the ground hard.

Still the Enforcer didn't make a move. Something was wrong with it, but Sasha wasn't about to complain. She didn't have time to think about what she was doing. She took a deep breath and climbed into the chair, moving slowly.

She had the headset in her hands when she heard his voice. 'Sasha!'

Her father.

She'd known he'd come. He couldn't stop her. She wouldn't let him.

She put the headset on. It was like a crown of thorns as it fastened in place. There was an intense surge of energy as she connected to the *Neuralnet*, the last remnant of something that had been happening when Buccaneer had been using it. It was so forceful it nearly blew her mind.

She had no idea what to do. 'Cal!' she called, but there was no response.

She tried to remember the last time she'd seen his face, but no matter how hard she tried she couldn't remember what he looked like. It was as if all her memories of him had slipped away. 'Cal?' It was no more than a whisper this time. But he was gone. Lost to her. Lost to the machine.

A man appeared in front of her: a tall man, a stranger. It wasn't Cal. She'd never seen him before in her life. Her father? She had no father. Did she? It was, wasn't it? Marshall Trent? Yes. No. She didn't know. Everything was getting jumbled up inside her head. Everything she thought she knew was being stripped away until there was only a small quiet voice calling to her. That voice she did recognise.

It was her own.

Her mind went blank.

Chapter 36

They kept low to the ground.

The trapdoor brought them out among a stand of elder and weeds. There were signs of old foundations where a building had once stood, but if you hadn't known it was there you would never have found it. Brambles snatched at them as they emerged into the bright daylight. Thorns clawed at their clothes and skin.

The air was full of the sound of Drones circling above them. Close. Too close for comfort.

Cal hoped that the Drones would not spot them huddling in the undergrowth, but with heat sensors and motion detectors he knew the chances of that were slim to none.

The entrance was close, but how could they reach it without giving their presence away?

Danni kept a finger pressed to her lips. He waited while she watched the skies, choosing her moment to break cover. She pointed out a pile of rubble less than fifty metres away, and gestured frantically. There was no mistaking the signal: run. But that meant crossing open ground. Then she was gone.

Cal froze. Up above the Drones gave no indication of deviating from their flight pattern. They were sweeping the area quadrant by quadrant.

He didn't have long. Seconds.

He burst out, running hard, arms and legs pumping furiously, eyes dead ahead, and didn't stop running until he reached Danni.

She held a grille open for him and he slipped through, landing knee-deep in water that seemed to be flowing quickly in both directions, even though that was impossible. The current pulled at his gown. Metal clanged on metal as she dropped the grille back into place, and splashed into the water beside him. The sounds echoed through the tunnel ahead and behind them.

Cal surged forward in the darkness, wishing they'd brought the lantern with them. Danni seemed unhindered by the dark. The water kept teasing open the back of his hospital gown. It would have been funny under normal circumstances, but not now. Now he just wanted to get to Sasha.

In the distance he saw a red glow. It grew brighter with each step and as they neared it solidified into a single red light above a metal door.

Danni pressed a series of buttons on a keypad beside the door. There was a click and a hiss as the lock was released, then it swung open. The light on the other side was a dull yellow. It reminded Cal of the disconnected datapods back in the *Neuralnet*.

He followed Danni inside, treading carefully as his feet squelched on the floor. He knew that they were inside the Anarchists' headquarters. He recognised it purely from the taste of the air. It was so different to the air outside, and yet so much better than the foetid dankness of the tunnels.

Danni raised her finger back to her lips, but he didn't need warning. She led the way along a corridor, past doors that began to look familiar. They were close to his mother's command room.

Cal knew that her body would be in there. He really didn't want to go in, but if Sasha was there . . . if she needed them . . . Danni rested her hand on the door handle, obviously wrestling the same fears. But they didn't have a choice; Danni pushed the door open.

In his mind he had prepared himself for the sight of his mother dead in the chair, but nothing could have prepared him for the reality. She wasn't in the chair at all. She was on the floor. There was someone else in the chair. Sasha. She was too small for the headset and she was slumped in the chair, her eyes lifeless. Cal suddenly felt physically sick. They were too late.

He'd failed her. She was dead and it was all his fault.

He stumbled towards the chair, distraught, even though that meant stepping over his mother's body. Tears streaked down his grubby face. The hospital gown billowed round his knees. He saw the rise and fall of Sasha's chest.

She was breathing.

His legs threatened to buckle beneath him as an overwhelming sense of relief flooded through him.

Then two things happened: he heard a chilling servo hiss and a muffled cry as the Enforcer moved lightning fast and pinned Danni, clamping a cold steel hand across her mouth so she couldn't make another sound. Then a voice said 'Hello, Callaghan.'

It wasn't Sasha.

It wasn't his mother.

He turned round, only to see a broken man emerge from the shadows. Marshall Trent. Beside him one of his Enforcers had Danni, waiting for the kill order to end the Anarchist uprising in its tracks. Danni didn't dare move. Her eyes were wide with absolute fear. 'What took you so long?'

'What have you done to her?' Cal demanded, meaning Sasha. He knew exactly what Marshall Trent had done to his mother.

'Me?' Trent said, seemingly surprised. 'I haven't done anything. This was all her.'

Cal didn't believe him. The man was stricken with grief. Something had snapped inside him after he'd done whatever he'd done to his daughter.

'What's wrong with you? You can't just leave her like that,' Cal started to yell at him.

'What do you expect me to do? I can't perform miracles, boy.'

'She needs a hospital.'

He shook his head. 'It's too late for that,' Trent said. 'She's only good for the datapods now. But that's your fault, isn't it?

You're the one who destroyed it all. Everything I worked so hard to build . . . the Isles I reunited . . . you tore it down in a day. You truly are your mother's son. I should have killed you the first time you crossed me.'

'This isn't my fault,' Cal said, looking at Sasha and really wanting that to be the truth.

'It's programmed into you. Hardwired to make you want to overthrow authority. Anarchy is in your blood. Just like your mother. That's what the chips were for. Without them we would never have been able to rebuild things so quickly. Without them we would still be fighting among ourselves. We needed a leader. We needed to know there was someone out there looking out for our interests. We needed to know that we were protected. That's all I ever did. I protected the weak. I was a shepherd. I protected my flock.'

'At the cost of your own daughter's life?' There was a flash of anger in Trent's eyes. Cal had had hit a raw nerve. 'What happened to her, Trent?'

'You.'

Cal shook his head. 'Not her. Your daughter. The *real* Sasha Trent.'

'She is the real Sasha Trent,' Trent said, clenching his right fist.

'No she isn't. The little girl who died eleven years ago was the real Sasha Trent.'

Chapter 37

What little fight he had left seemed to leech out of Marshall Trent as Cal revealed his secret was no longer secret. A sucker punch to the gut wouldn't have been more effective. Trent shrank in on himself while the Enforcer stood mutely beside him

'Does it matter?' Trent said at last. A single tear broke and ran down his cheek.

Cal reached out and the man flinched, backing away as if afraid that Cal was going to hit him, but all he did was take hold of the man's rig. That was how he accessed the *Neuralnet*. Cal had no idea if there was anything left to contact.

He looked at Danni. She was desperately trying to shake her head, fear in her eyes, but he had to do this.

'I'll come back,' he said, and connected Trent's rig to the *Neuralnet*. He felt a surge as he made contact, but it was nothing like the sudden rush that had accompanied his last uplink in the Watchhouse. The headset Sasha wore would have provided him with a more direct connection – and perhaps a more powerful one – but he wasn't about to remove it until he knew Sasha was out of the system and safe. He wasn't going to lose her the same way he'd lost his mother.

He felt around inside his mind for the tiny flickers that were all that remained of the *Neuralnet*. The rig offered the same kind of access his own scavenged rig had offered. He wasn't a god in here now. There were no gods in this place, only faded and burnt-out lights too weak for him to tap into.

Was there anything left in here that could help him? Something he could use to turn the remaining Enforcers to his advantage?

Outside, the Drones circled. He tried to connect with the rest of Trent's mechanoid army. They were up there, waiting. Only one had ventured inside with Trent. Its presence felt like a threat, but to who, Trent or Cal? It hadn't tried to stop Cal. He couldn't connect with its default program and now the *Neuralnet* had collapsed he wasn't getting any help from the machine. Even so, he could feel that there was something fundamentally *wrong* with this Enforcer.

The Enforcers gave him the creeps. This one stood in silence. Watching. Waiting.

A question formed in his mind. *How are the Enforcers controlled?*

He wasn't expecting an answer, but detailed schematics flooded his mind. He saw the blueprints of a separate portion of an operating system that was shielded from the Black Flag virus, a quarantined part of the machine cut off from anything, which could shut it down once and for all. How many pods were still running the machine? One, ten, one hundred? What were they capable of, these last few wretched souls tied into the machine?

Answers scrolled past him, details of everything he could ever have wanted to know about the Enforcers and the Drones, every question he could ever have imagined and more he couldn't. Not only were they able to restrain and kill they were capable of healing the injured and possessed diagnostic equipment built into their metal bodies that made them living computers in their own right. That was how the *Neuralnet* was surviving, he realised. It was in them and they were in it. Inseparable.

Who is this girl? Cal framed the thought, directing his question to the Enforcer that still held Danni immobile without actually voicing it. It could hear him.

Analysis in progress.

Cal waited as the Enforcer released Danni and moved across to Sasha's unmoving body to complete its assessment, drawing a tiny amount of blood that it would process inside its built in lab.

Danni ran to stand beside Cal.

Initial scan indicates that the remains of the Neurochip in her skull was registered to one Sasha Trent.

But who is Sasha Trent?

DNA assessment has resulted in familial matches. Data being accessed. There is a genetic match between three bodies in this room.

Three? Who?

The images appeared inside his head, side by side. One was his mother, a little younger. It was time-stamped 2073. Eleven years ago.

There was a little girl with her. And beside them both, Cal. That meant that the girl slumped in the chair was his sister.

'My sister?' he said out loud, unable to stop the words coming to his lips.

'Almost,' Trent said.

Cal looked up from the rig.

'She's a clone of your mother grown to replace the daughter I lost.'

'But why? Why would you do that?'

'Because we could. Because your mother knew how to. Because she was able to safeguard Sasha's memories, her hopes and dreams, her personality, and give me my little girl back. We made a copy of everything before she died. Once the body reached four years, the same age my Sasha was when she was taken from me, we wiped the clone's mind and replaced her memories with those we'd stored. Your mother gave me my little girl back. It was the best gift she could ever have given me. It's why I let your mother live . . . even when she tried to take it all back . . .' Trent said, trailing off.

'I don't believe you,' Cal said automatically, but the evidence was overwhelming. In a matter of hours he'd lost the mother he'd only just rediscovered and found a sister who, right now, was dying right in front of his very eyes.

'He's telling the truth,' Danni said.

Cal turned to look at her. 'You knew?'

'Buccaneer told me everything,' Danni said. 'She needed someone she could trust.'

'And it's true? All of it . . .? I mean . . .?'

Danni nodded.

Will she be all right? Cal asked the Enforcer through the connection on the rig.

Her life signs are good. She will recover. Physically.

That didn't mean she'd be the same Sasha when he pulled her out of the *Neuralnet*. But he couldn't leave her in there. The machine was dying.

He searched the forest of pale lights. If her mind was still connected to the system, he'd find her. It was as simple as that. He wasn't breaking the connection until he'd got her out of there. She was his sister. If she was lost it was his job to find her. That was how it worked. They were family.

Where are you? he thought. *Sasha? Can you hear me? Where are you? I'm here. I'm coming to find you. Let me know where you are. Help me find you. Sasha? Please. You're safe, I promise.*

There was a glow in the forest of yellow, a pale pink that stood out against the background. It was different to the rest of the stagnant data streams. There was still a pulse of life in it. Soon there'd be nothing left.

Cal ran towards the light. He heard the sound of crying long before he reached her.

The sobbing grew louder as he approached. Curled among a cluster of yellow trees that seemed more benign than inert, a small girl sat on the floor, her arms wrapped round her knees. She was rocking herself and crying. She had her eyes closed.

Cal recognised her. It was his sister. His mother's cloned child. Yes it was Sasha, but at the same time it wasn't. This was the girl she had been, the little sister he had lost: restored to the limited memories she had had before her mind had been wiped to make way for Marshall Trent's dead daughter. He had to get her out of there. He had to protect her. On a very basic level that's what brothers did.

'Open your eyes,' Cal said softly, and held out his hand for her to take.

Chapter 38

Cal had followed the Enforcer as it took Marshall Trent back to the halls of the living computer.

Kit was still tending to the bodies that were alive inside the datapods. One of them was painfully familiar. Cal stood beside Kit as he cared for his father. His father's eyes were closed and Kit was feeding him through a straw.

'Can you help him?'

'I don't know,' Kit admitted. 'Some of them are waking up. Some aren't. It depends if he's still in there, or if the mind wipe was complete . . . If it was . . . then even if he does wake up he won't even remember how to function as a human being. I'm sorry.'

'Don't let him go,' Cal said. 'I'm not ready to lose him.'

Kit couldn't look at him. 'I'll keep him connected to the machine, and care for him and the others, while I wait for them to wake up. We can only hope that they will. One day. Now that the net's failed there's nothing connecting them. But they've got to learn how to live for themselves again. Some might not make it. But I'll look after them, I promise.' And that was all he had ever done, tend to and care for the people who made up the machine.

Kit moved away, leaving the family alone.

'Thank you,' Cal said, tears glistening in his eyes.

Cal leaned forward and kissed his father's forehead. 'Open your eyes, Dad. Please. I've got someone here who really wants to meet you. All you've got to do is open your eyes. Please, Dad, just open your eyes.'

There was a beep, deep within the machine. A flicker in his father's vital signs.

'Open your eyes.'

Another beep. And another. Faster. More urgent.

Cal gripped his hand. 'Open your eyes,' he said again.

The girl beside him took Cal's other hand, and repeated what her brother was saying. She hadn't changed physically, she was still the same Sasha Trent who had rebelled against her father Marshall Trent. She looked the same in every way that mattered. The only difference was in the sparkle behind her eyes. Her eyes looked so much *younger* than her face. That was reinforced by the peculiar innocence in the way she copied him, but then she was learning how to be herself again and only had four years' worth of memories, so of course she mimicked him. It would take a long time for her to become the young woman she was always meant to be. But Cal would be with her every step of the way. He'd tell her stories about how she'd risked everything to stand up for people who couldn't stand up for themselves and bring to life adventures she'd never remember, and in return she'd tell him stories about yesterday and last week, things they'd done with their mother that he'd completely forgotten because to him it had happened so long ago. And together they'd learn exactly who they were. They had all the time in the world. Cal squeezed Sasha's hand a little bit tighter.

'Open your eyes. Open your eyes. Open your eyes.'

And then he did.

It took Cal's father a moment to focus. His lips moved, but his voice was so weak, his mouth so parched and brittle, that Cal couldn't hear what he said until he leaned in so closely that he could feel his father's fluttering breath against his ear. 'You found her.' He could have meant his mother or his sister; it didn't matter.

Cal nodded. He wanted to tell his father to rest, to save his strength and to get better, because he knew exactly what being inside one of those datapods for a week did to you, and his father had been inside at least a week longer than Cal had. He could see him struggling to put together thoughts, to remember who he was. There were blank patches where the words didn't exist yet, but his vocabulary would return second by second. He struggled to put words to concepts, big things like pride and justice and love, but they came together.

His father said, 'She loved you . . . you know that, don't you?'

Cal nodded again. 'My eyes are wide open,' he promised.

'I tried to help . . . in there . . . when you were all alone . . . I tried to show you her . . . I wanted you to remember who she was . . . I just wish I could have done more . . . I loved her so much . . . I love you so much . . . every time I look at you I see her . . .'

Suddenly Cal understood why that picture of his mother had kept coming up in those first searches when he couldn't even remember himself. He'd always assumed his dad's coldness towards her meant he had never loved his mother. He was wrong. He'd loved her so very much and had been heartbroken by her leaving. That was why he'd never talked about her. And in that his mum had been wrong, he never would have turned her over to Marshall Trent, no matter how much he believed in peace.

Cal's father smiled. It was a tragic smile. The strap across his forehead stopped him from buckling and falling forward. 'You did it, son,' he said, his voice getting stronger as he squeezed Sasha's hand.

'This is Sasha,' Cal said. 'My sister.'

His father looked at her, seeming to see her for the first time. Perhaps he'd thought she was a ghost beside him? Some remnant of the machine haunting his waking mind?

'I always wondered what kind of girl you'd grow up to be. Maybe now I'll find out. You look just like her when she was your age . . .'

'Where's Mummy?' Sasha asked, breaking Cal's heart a little bit.

'She's watching over us,' their father promised.

Chapter 39

They emerged from the Watchhouse into the bright light of a brand-new day.

It was the first of many to come.

Cal and Sasha were hand-in-hand, Danni beside Cal, his father and Kit behind.

Survivors.

All around the plaza Cal saw people moving aimlessly, an emptiness inside them where the *Neuralnet* had been. It took him a moment to realise what it was he saw in their faces: fear. They were so unused to the freedom of their own minds, they didn't know how to think. Or at least some of them didn't. In the distance he could see the smoking ruins of an Enforcer's shell where it had been burned out by gangs from one of the Communities. They must have been the first to open their eyes and understand just what it all meant, what had been done to them, how Marshall Trent had ruled their lives with fear and propaganda, and now they wanted to tear down everything that reminded them of his oppressive rule. That was his legacy.

'Can you feel it? It's changed,' his father said. 'Everything's changed. You did that, son. It's a brand-new world now.'

He could feel it. 'People are so used to being connected,' he said. 'It doesn't matter what machine it is, what kind of computer rig or *Neuralnet*, the one fundamental truth of our life has always been that people need people and will do anything to feel a part of a greater whole. That's why everyone embraced the machine. It made them feel connected.'

'And now they don't,' Danni said. 'And that's because of us. We're responsible for that.'

It was hard to argue with that. They'd all but destroyed the machine. Danni had worked out how to neutralise the

195

Neurochips and give them a chance at freedom, and together they'd pulled the plug on the *Neuralnet*, burning out the interfaces in everyone's heads when they'd triggered the Black Flag program and demanded that everyone open their eyes.

They walked through the plaza together, heading back towards the Community.

He had no idea if the old house would be standing.

If it wasn't, then side-by-side with everyone else they would build something from the rubble.

'What happens now?' Cal asked. He'd been thinking about it a lot over the last few hours, as the reality of what they'd done began to sink in. He hadn't had time to grieve yet, that would come. Everything had happened so fast and it finally felt like he could breathe. It was a big question. It wasn't just a 'now we go and get something to eat' kind of question. It meant everything.

'The world's broken. Someone will come along and fix it,' his father said. 'That's what always happens. That's how Marshall Trent happened. He came when we needed him. Now someone else will come. That's just the way the world works.'

Cal shook his head. 'Then we'll end up with someone like Trent, won't we? That means everything will have been for nothing.'

Danni nodded. 'If the world needs rebuilding, it's our responsibility. We did this. We fix it.'

Cal thought about that for a moment. Without the *Neuralnet* it would be difficult, but not impossible, but then the true meaning of what she was saying struck him. He shook his head again. 'No, that's what went wrong before. We can't do this alone. It's everyone's responsibility . . . We're all in this together, otherwise we'll just repeat the same mistakes. Right now it's a world of possibility. It's up to us to make sure everyone makes the most of it.'

Danni took his free hand and smiled at him.

'It's amazing what you can do dressed in a hospital gown with half your bum hanging out.'

Sasha laughed at that.

The four of them walked hand-in-hand into a bright future.

Chapter 40

The Enforcer took Marshall Trent into the quarantined sector.

There was only one Enforcer now. The rest had been destroyed when they'd run out of fuel and fallen from the skies after spending too long in the air circling in search of Sasha, following orders that no one had rescinded. They couldn't stop looking. It wasn't in their programming.

The last Enforcer led Marshall Trent into the depths of the cellars where the mainframe – the single computer that was, in essence, the very core of the *Neuralnet* – was stored. A datapod stood open ready for him. It was all that remained of the great machine that had connected every single Citizen. Now it would be Marshall Trent's prison.

He tried to fight it at first, knowing that a fate worse than death was waiting for him once that glass door closed, but no matter how desperately he struggled he couldn't stop the Enforcer, and, no matter how much he begged, it would carry out its orders.

Cal came into the room and closed the door behind him.

'Save me. Please. You've got to. You're not like me. You can't do this,' Marshall Trent pleaded.

'Save you?' Cal thought about it. 'I could. Perhaps we could make a deal . . .?'

'Yes. Anything. Anything you want. It's yours. Just name it.'

'Give me my mother back and we'll call it even.'

The hope died in Marshall Trent's eyes. 'I can't . . .' He shook his head, and started to fight against the Enforcer's restraints. 'She's gone. Something else. Anything else. It's yours. The Isles? They're yours. You can be a king! I can make you a king!'

'You're wrong, Trent,' Cal said. 'She's not gone. I found her, or rather a back-up of her. She was clever like that. She planned

198

ahead. She always knew this day would come. She's waiting for you in there. Give her my love, won't you?'

'Please . . . don't do this. You don't have to do this.'

'I do,' Cal said. 'I really do.'

With that, the Enforcer sealed the datapod, trapping Marshall Trent inside.

He lashed about, fighting hopelessly against the cords that snaked down in search of his neural interface.

In the silence of the machine, only the ghost of Buccaneer could hear him scream.

Puzzle Answers

Some of the challenges you will face on the companion website are quite difficult. Do not worry if you are unable to solve all of them – you are just beginning your training. If you get really stuck with a puzzle, the password you require is given below (well, almost).

The passwords and passphrases have been encrypted to avoid you accidentally seeing the answers to puzzles you haven't attempted yet. All of the letters in the passwords have been encrypted using a Caesar Cipher, each with a different shift. For example, the "Hidden Login" puzzle's passphrase has had all of its letters shifted 7 places like this:

plain alphabet: a b c d e f g h i j k l m n o p q r s t u v w x y z
cipher alphabet: H I J K L M N O P Q R S T U V W X Y Z A B C D E F G

Numbers, symbols and spaces are unaltered.

To obtain the passphrase or password for a particular puzzle, you will need to decode the encrypted version given here. This is done by setting up two alphabets, just as we have done above, but each puzzle requires a different shift. Once you have done this, you will simply have to replace all of the capital letters with their corresponding lowercase ones.

The second puzzle you will encounter in your training will involve creating scripts that make the task of decoding these answers much easier.

Hidden Login	KVDU AOL YHIIPA OVSL	(shift = 7)
Caesar Cipher	O = N - PJD	(shift = 5)
Cal's PID	2JGJXWMBZJLEJWJOK	(shift = 6)
Infernal Noise	NJGQZ OCZ KPUUGZN	(shift = 21)
Fibonacci's Rabbits	8670007398507948658051921	
Caesar Cipher Solver	RMNDUOMFUAZ	(shift = 12)
Super Caesar Cipher	UGEXGJLSTDW	(shift = 18)
Fractal Tree	1023	
Open Your Eyes	780	
Dictionary Search	SPCCXRPXC	(shift = 15)
Drone Scan	280,560	
Memory Maps	ALD	(shift = 23)

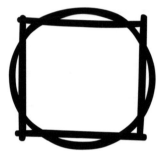

Open your eyes...